IN LOVE with the PLANET

Photos & Stories

CATHRYN WELLNER

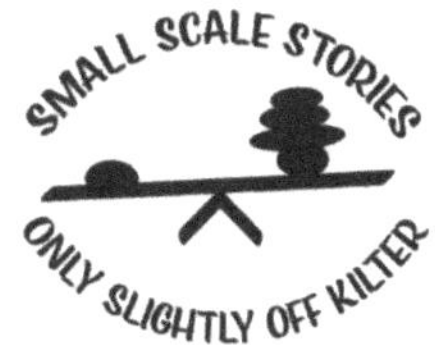

Small Scale Stories #9
Espoir Press
British Columbia 2019

Espoir Press
1002 - 1128 Sunset Drive
Kelowna, British Columbia
Canada V1Y 9W7

©2019 Cathryn Wellner

In Love with the Planet (Small Scale Stories #9)

ISBN 978-1-988760-17-9

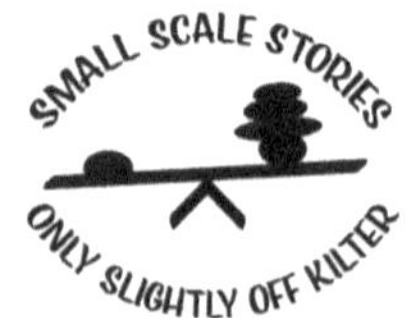

SO EXQUISITE

A reflection catches your eye. You stand in awe.

A rock is so ancient you wonder what it has seen. You stop and listen for its stories.

Flowers grow in an unlikely spot. You see in them the miracle of life.

A rose looks wonky, asymmetrical. You honor its beauty.

Your friend forgets the words to a song. You sing them for him.

You, my friend, are a planet lover. You hear the songs of wind, earth, people, and water. You love knowing you contain within you the same elements as the stars of the Milky Way. You feel your connection with geese, trees, ants, and clouds. You know a secret others overlook, that every rock, duck, leaf, and even building, is your relative. You stretch your arms and heart to embrace them all.

The Small Scale Stories in this ninth entry in the series are for you. You are helping to safeguard this exquisite planet.

Share the stories with friends. Some people will scratch their heads and find you strange. But your tribe, your planet-loving friends, will be happy to know they are not alone.

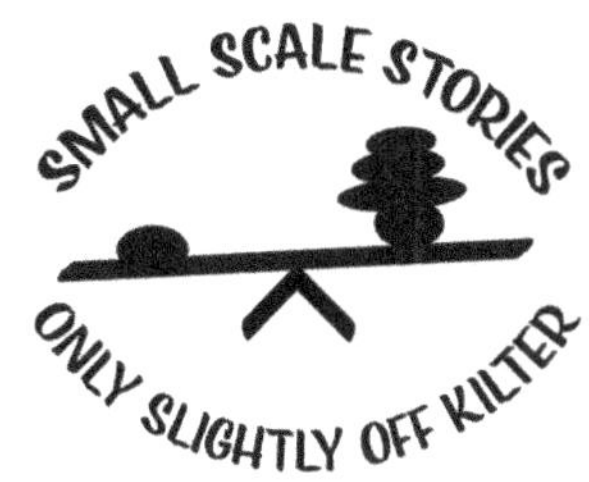

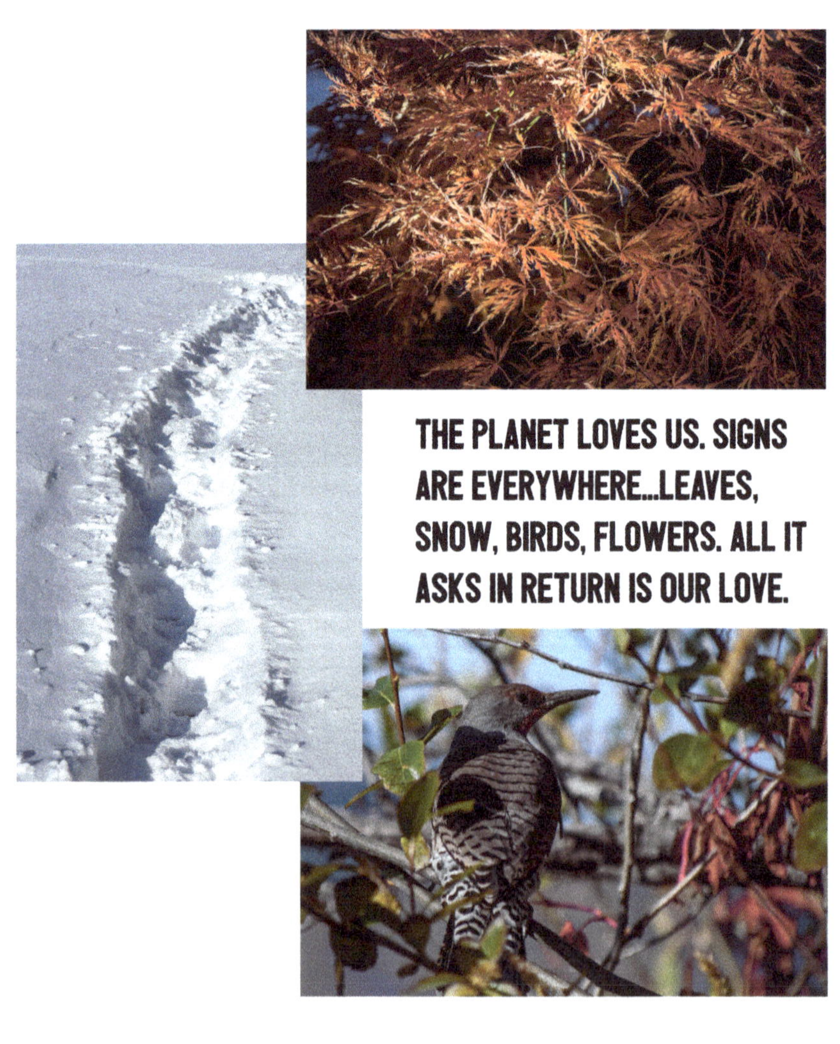
THE PLANET LOVES US. SIGNS
ARE EVERYWHERE...LEAVES,
SNOW, BIRDS, FLOWERS. ALL IT
ASKS IN RETURN IS OUR LOVE.

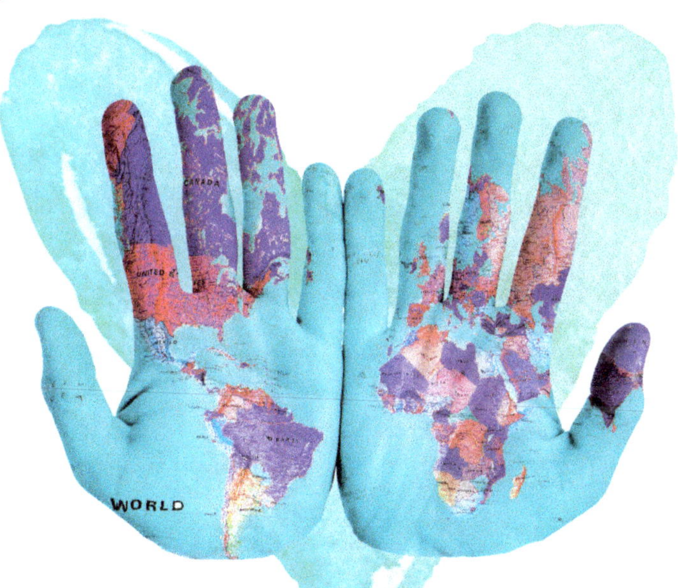

THE PLANET
IS IN YOUR HANDS
LOVE
LOVE IT WITH ALL YOUR HEART
WORLD

THE STORIES

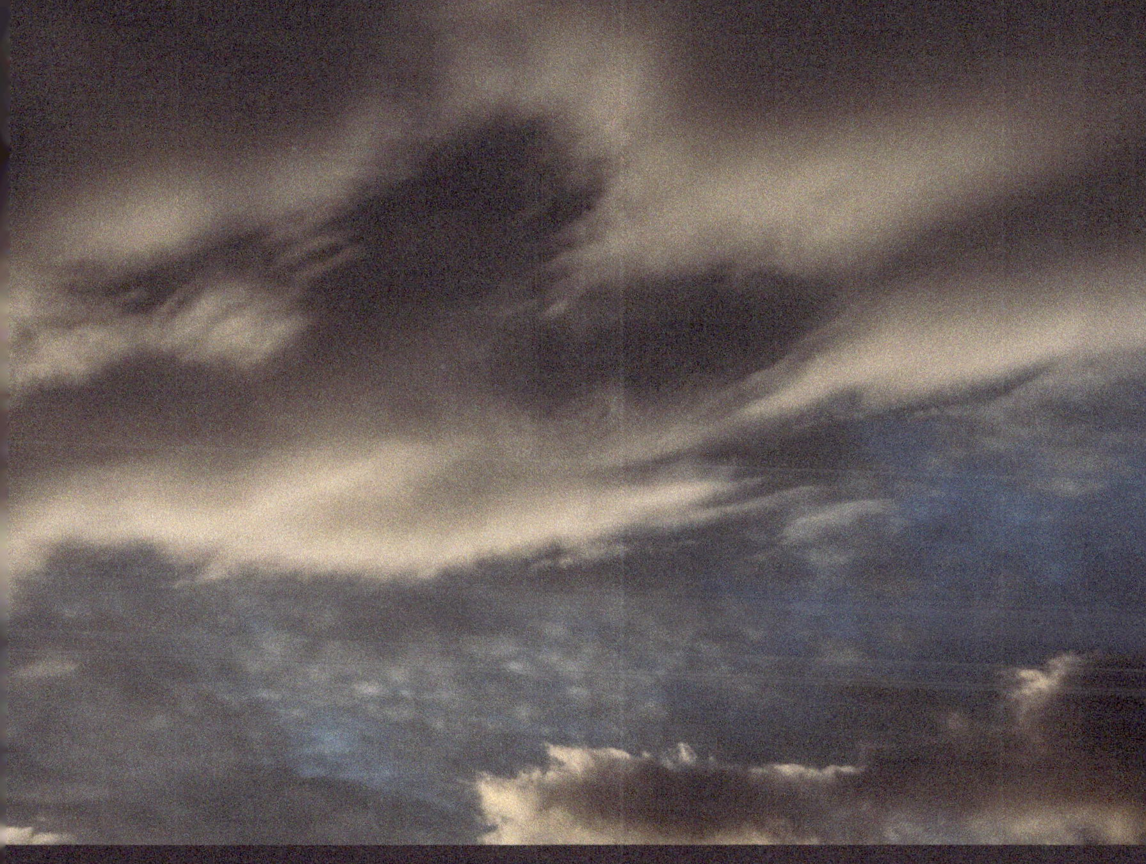

Clouds were in love with the planet. Sometimes they just had to show how much they adored the land and water below them.

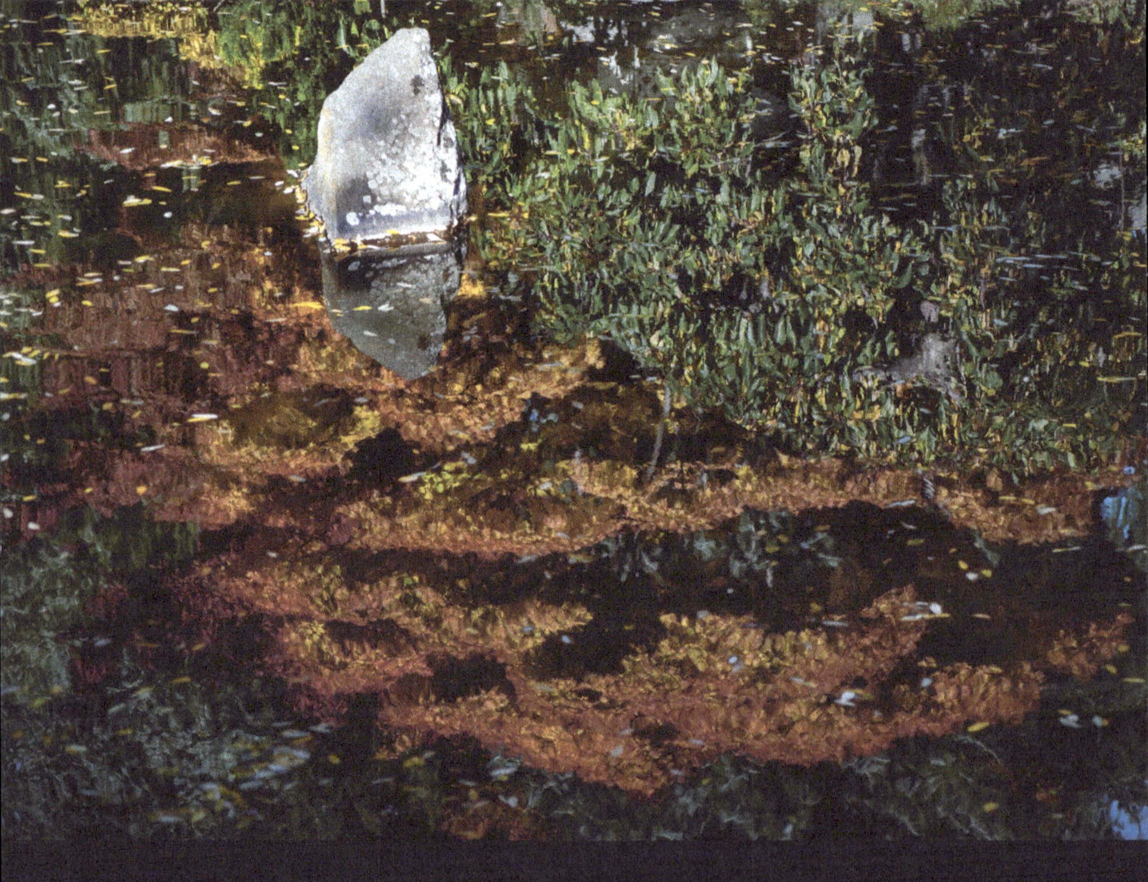

Leaves gathered around to listen. Even the reflections paid attention. Stone was the best storyteller in the pond. He knew about seasons and change and told fascinating tales.

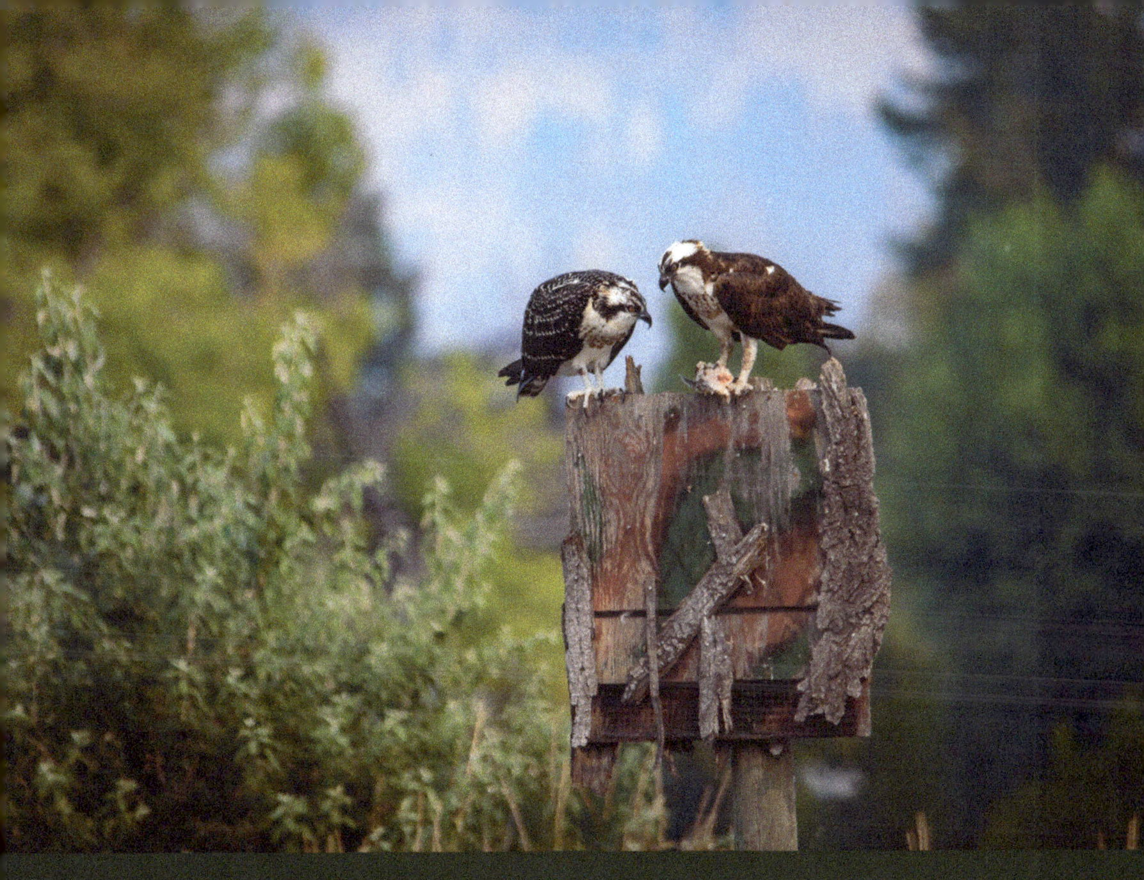

"You know I love you, Junior, but we'll be migrating soon. It's time you learned to feed yourself."

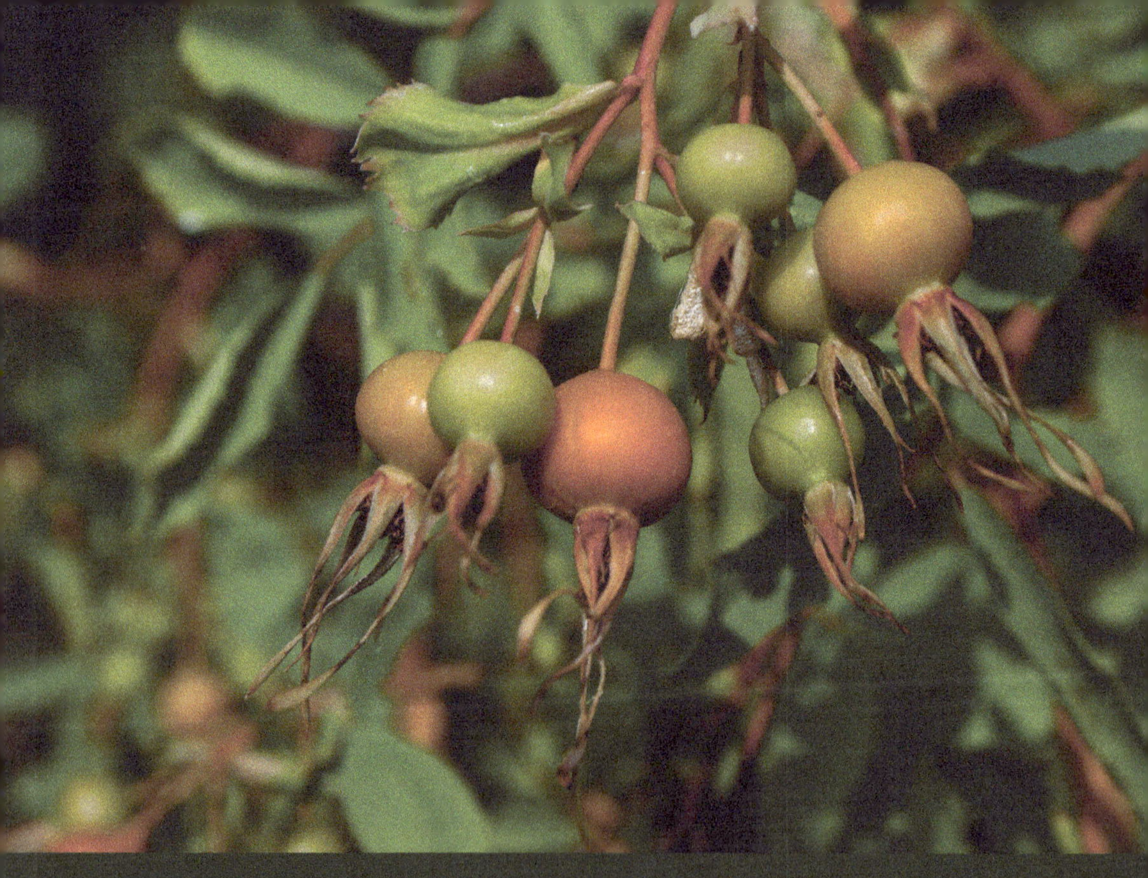

Big Red listened to the silly jokes of the Small Greens and the wistful conversation of the Mid-Oranges. She could offer sage advice on the stages remaining in their lives. Better yet, she could listen and encourage and love.

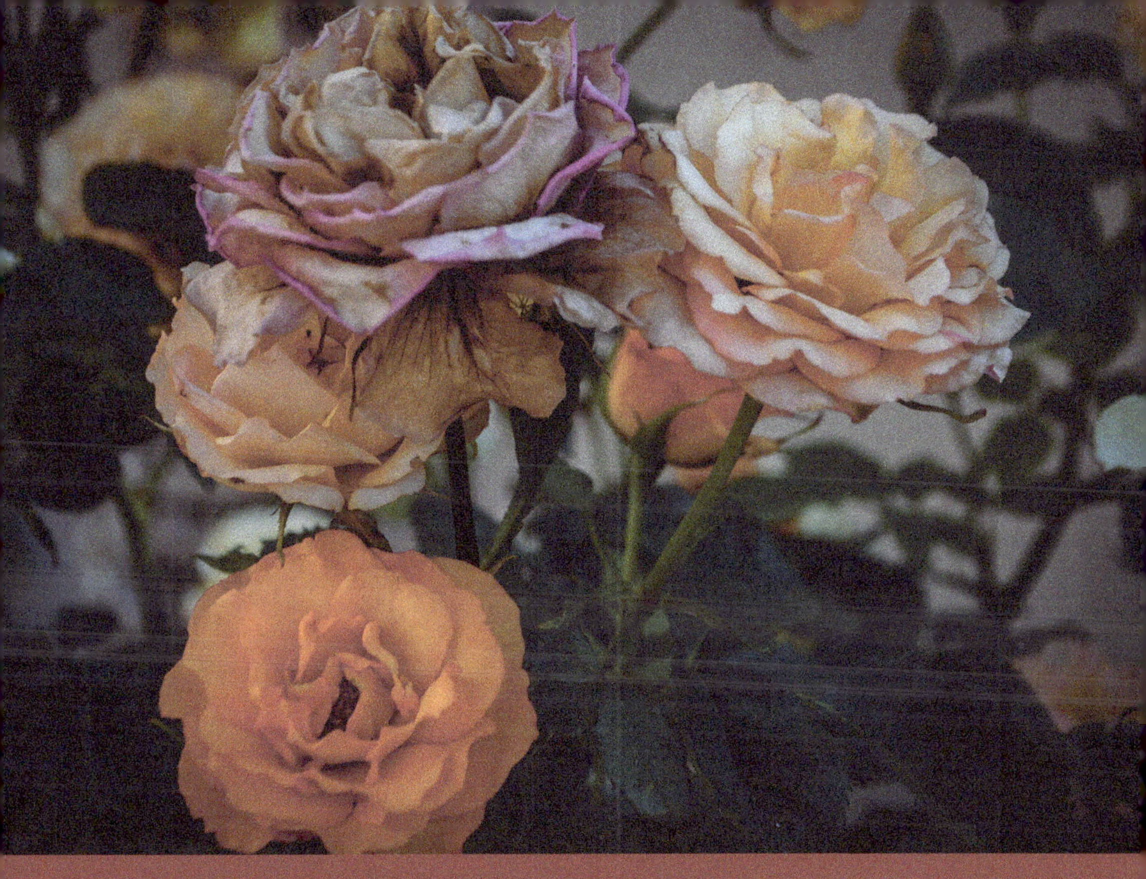

Three generations clustered around the oldest rose. They listened to her stories, wondered at her wisdom, and prepared to say goodbye.

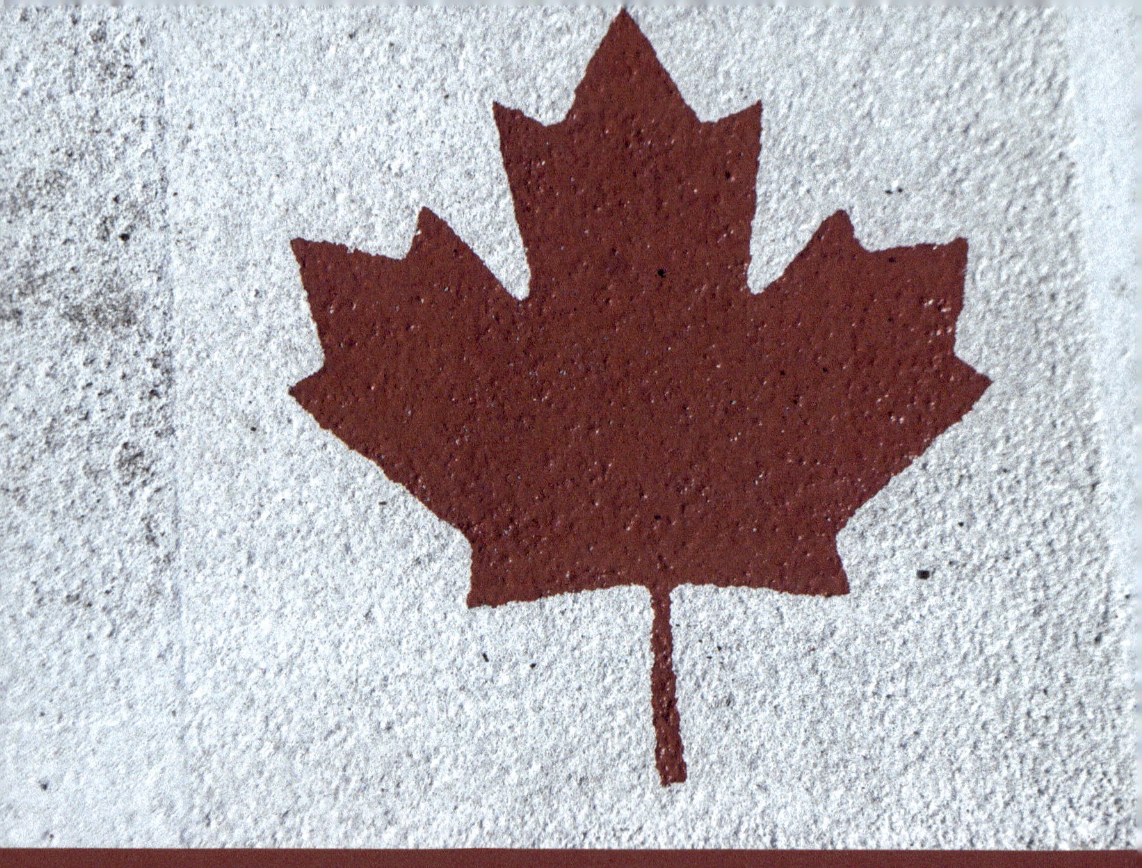

The City People painted Leaf just before Canada Day. She glowed with quiet pride. Tires began rolling over the walkway where she lay. They ground dirt into her, but she never forgot the glory of her special day.

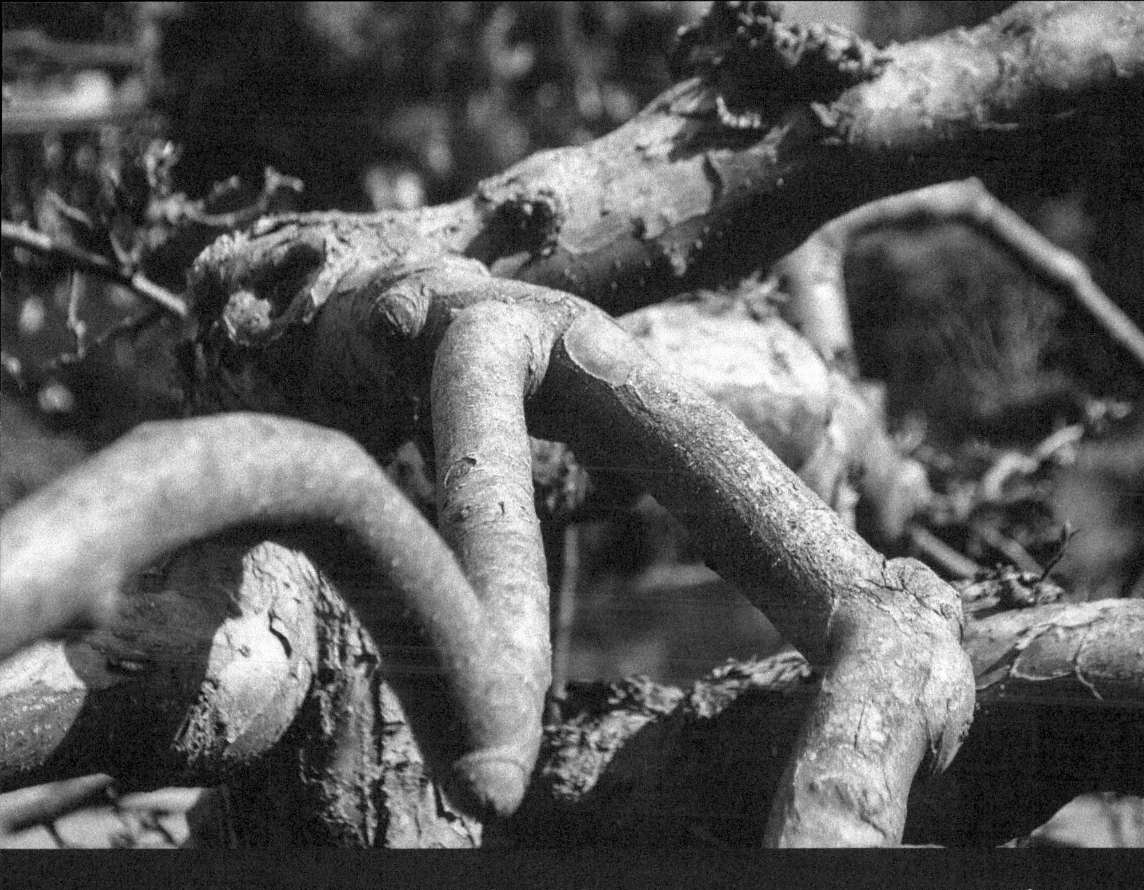

Tree Golum rested his head on Tree Snoopy. With the garden open for summer, they would fall silent during visiting hours. Only when the gates closed would they continue telling their frightening or hilarious stories.

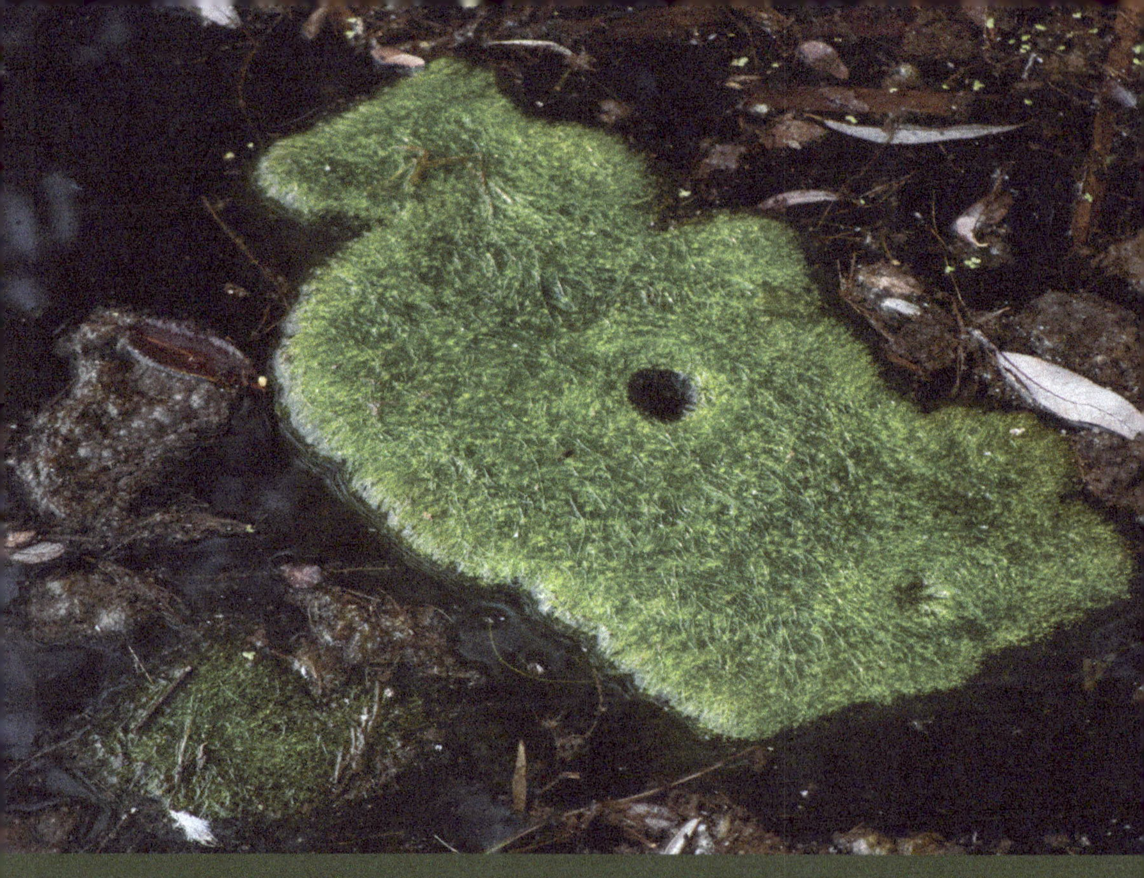

The algae considered themselves artists, which to them meant freedom from creative restraints. They shaped a seahorse head, two grizzly humps, the belly of a pregnant camel, and a bum like a green border collie, then added a perfect hole.

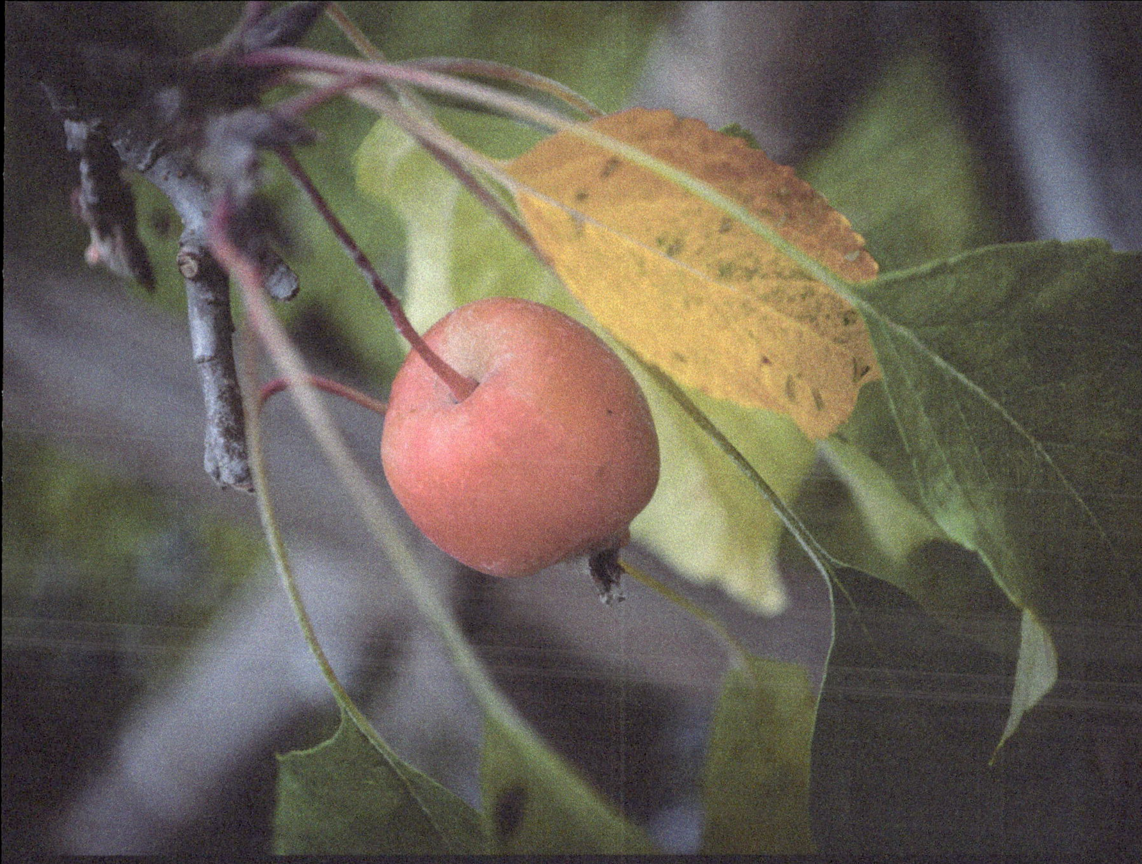

Crabapple was lonely. Her friends were gone. She had no idea what happened to them, beyond the gossip of leaves and limbs. Their stories made her shiver, but being completely alone bothered her more than the prospect of being eaten.

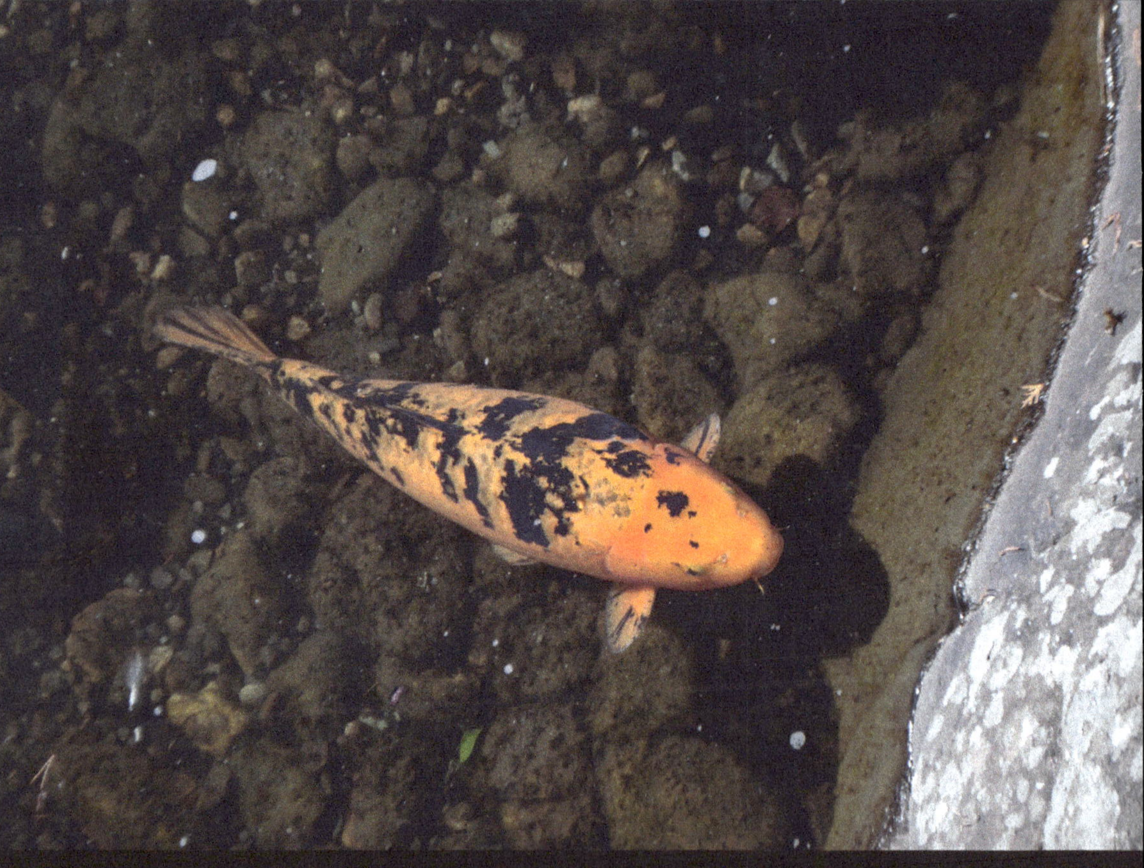

"I've hit a wall," thought Koi, staring at the impenetrable surface in front of him. "What a good place to rest while I contemplate my next move." Although he had never hit a wall before, he knew in time he would figure out what to do.

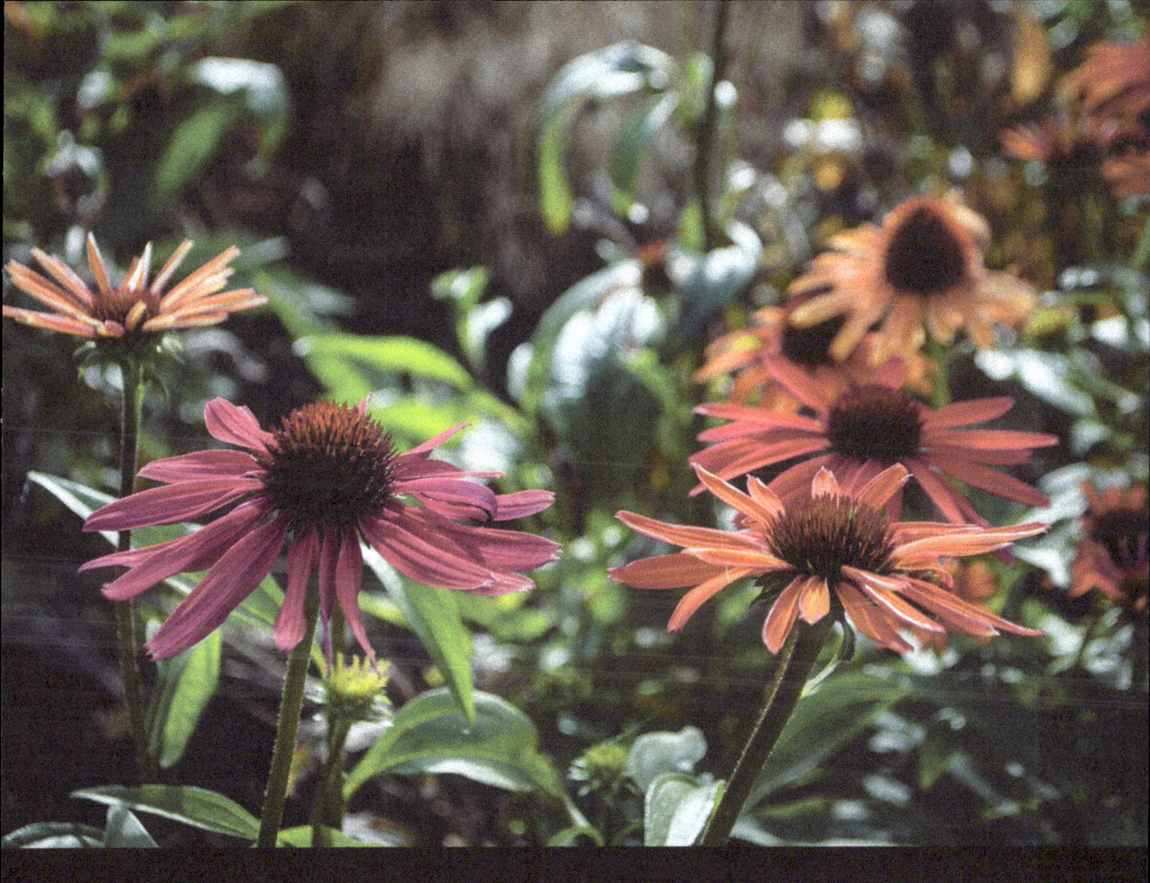

Well into autumn, the coneflowers still wore their finery. As each flower faded, those still lively would sing to them, a song of love and farewell and sweet memories.

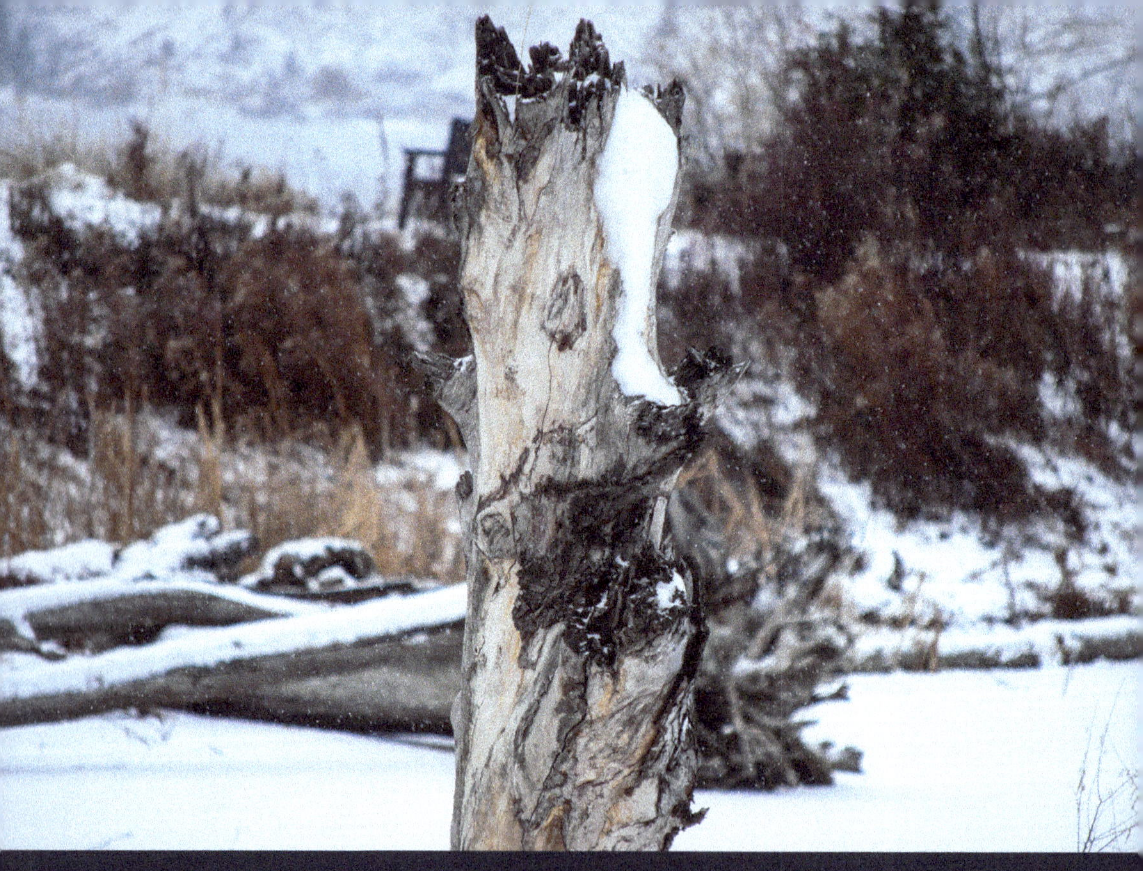

Roscoe was thrilled with the snow. He had been trying to imitate a pony head. Finally he had a blaze. Now his pals would see his clever disguise.

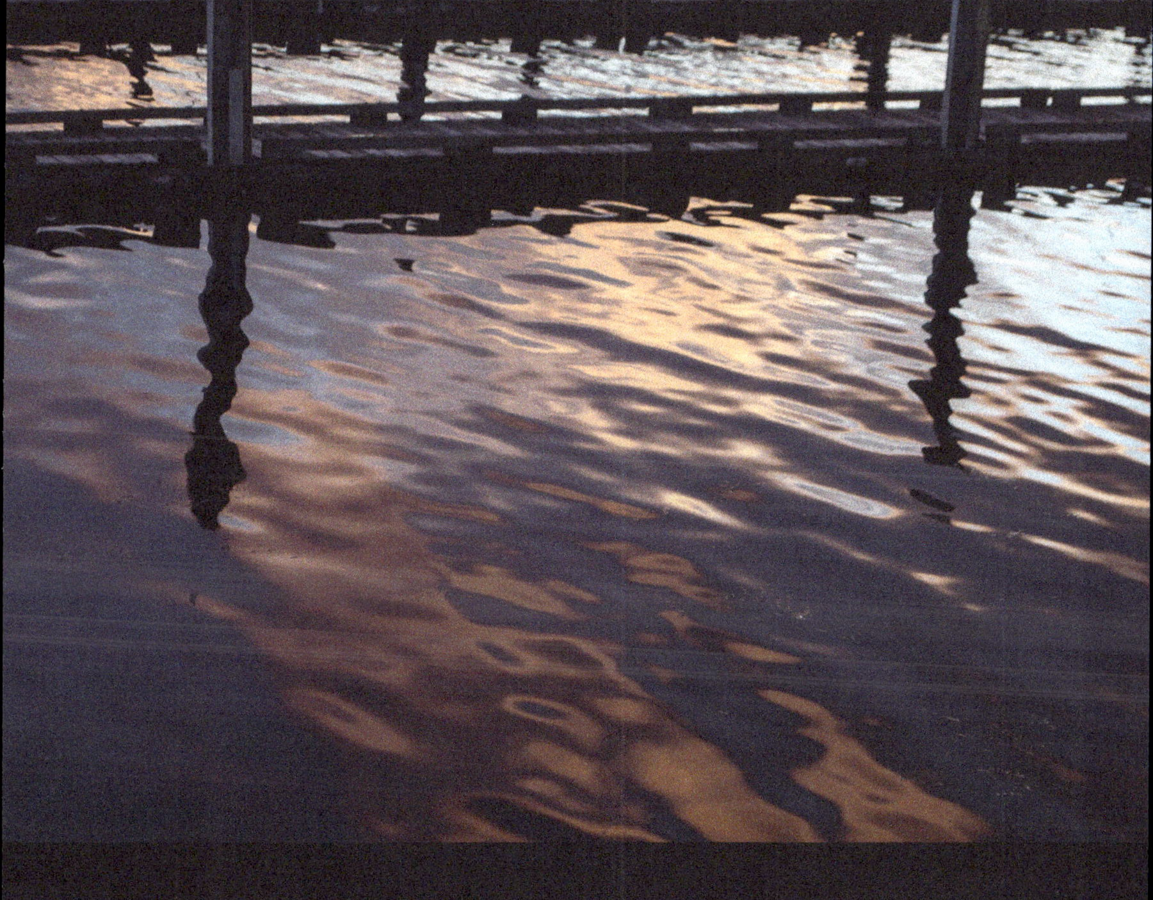

Water and Dock were reminiscing when Wind swept down to say hello. That put a whole new wrinkle in the conversation.

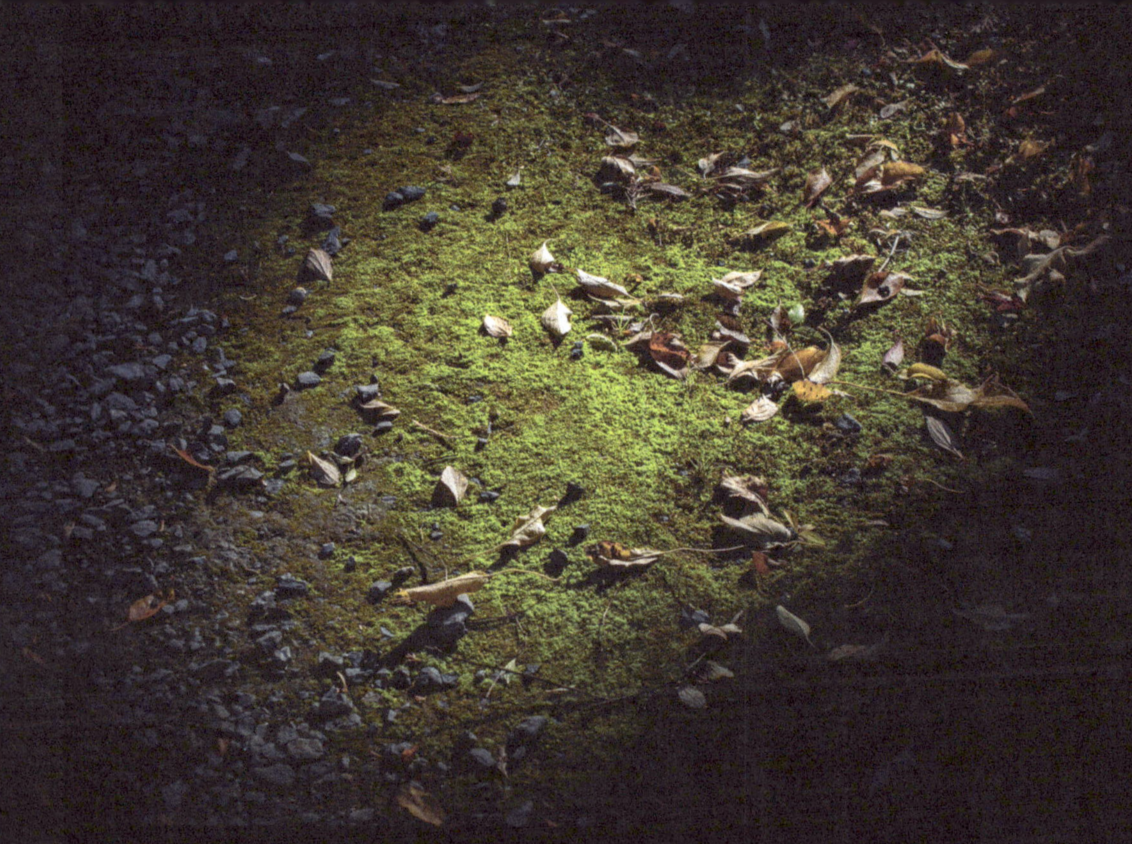

As afternoon shadows lengthened, Sun sent a heart to show the falling leaves and the passersby the love he felt for the soft, green moss.

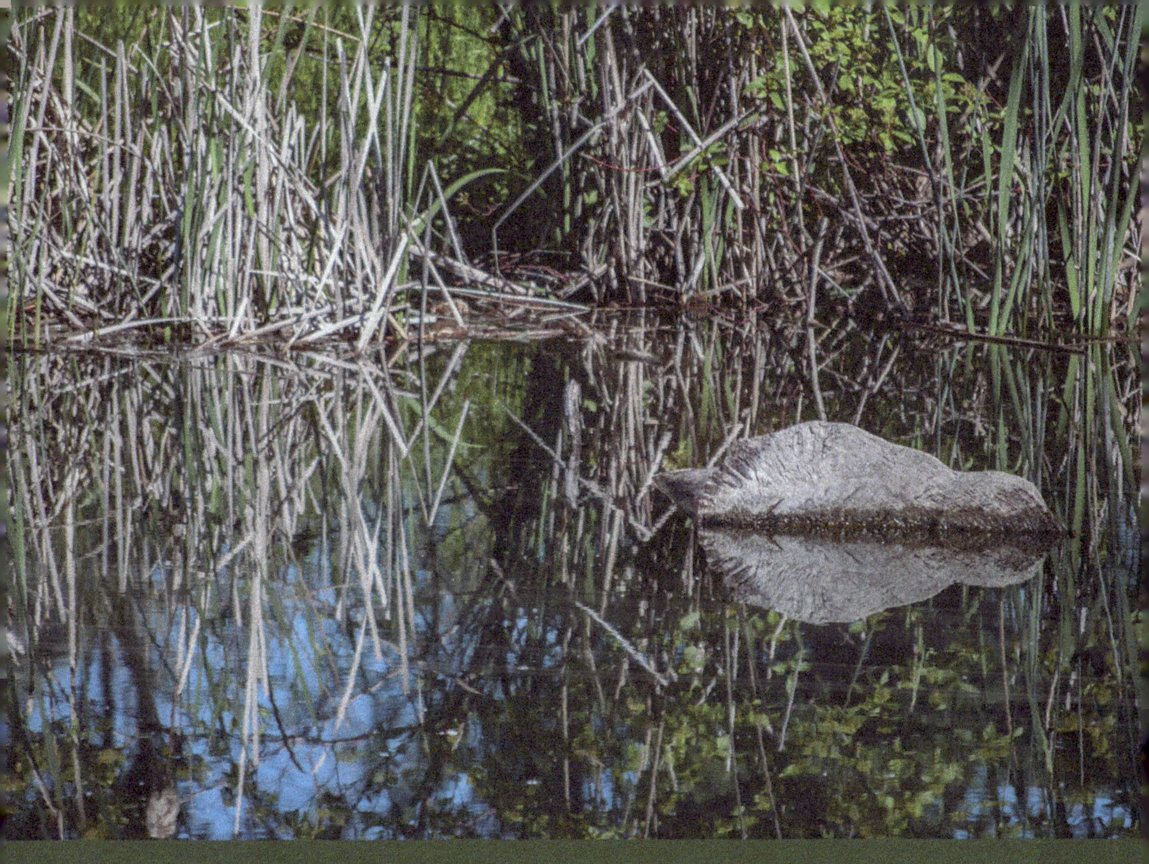

Log's pals, the turtles and ducks, abandoned him when the water rose. There were compensations, however. On still days, he and Water played reflection games. Today they were a plump seal, lying on her side.

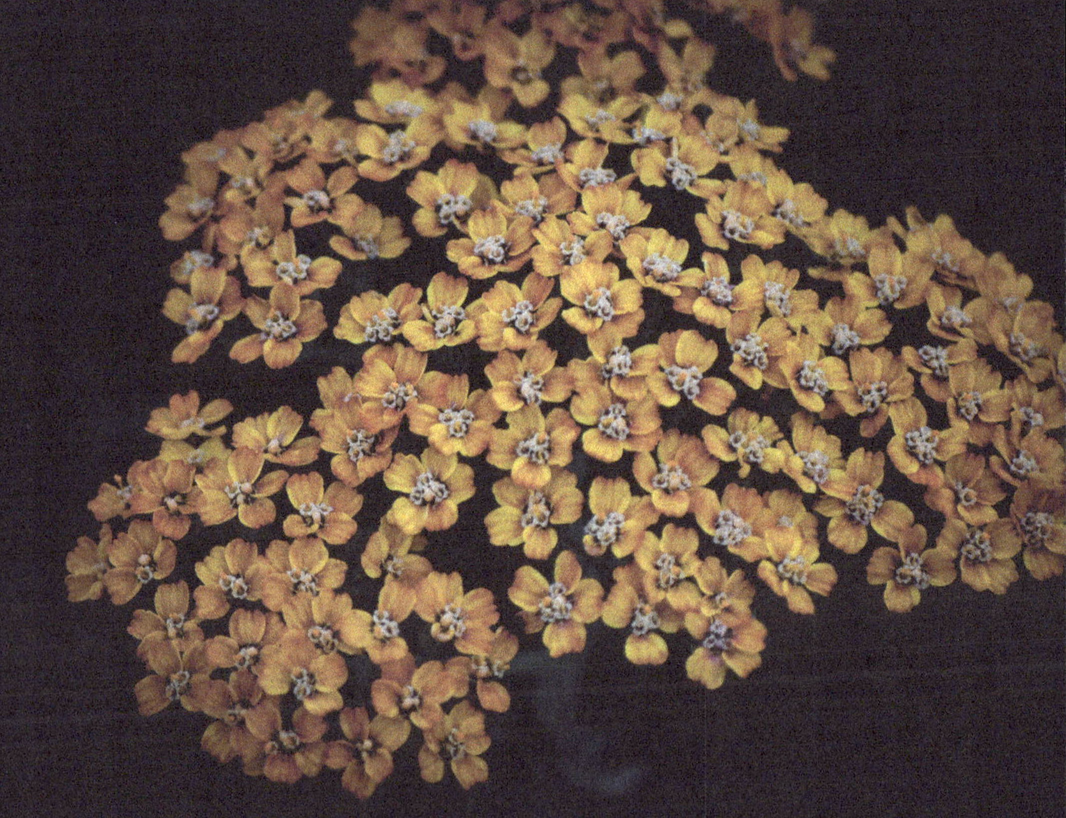

They loved hearing people exclaim how beautiful they were. "Imagine!" the people would say. "They are growing by the police station. I wonder if the people in jail can see and enjoy them?" Flowers knew the inmates couldn't and felt sad for them.

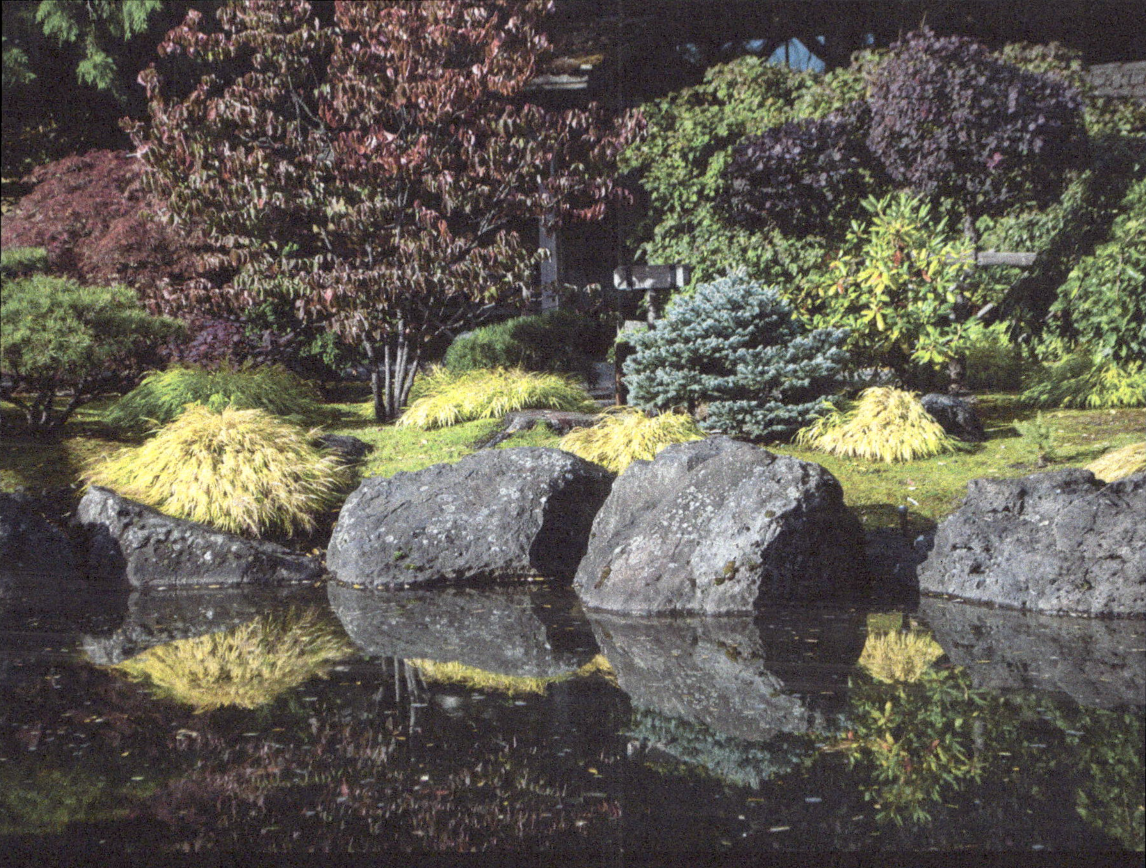

The quiet stones and lively reflections talked about the summer just ended. They missed Slider, the turtle who hibernated at the first hint of cold. They wished the flashy koi were more active when the water cooled. Trees and bushes reminded them of the rowdy parties they'd have when the garden gates closed for winter.

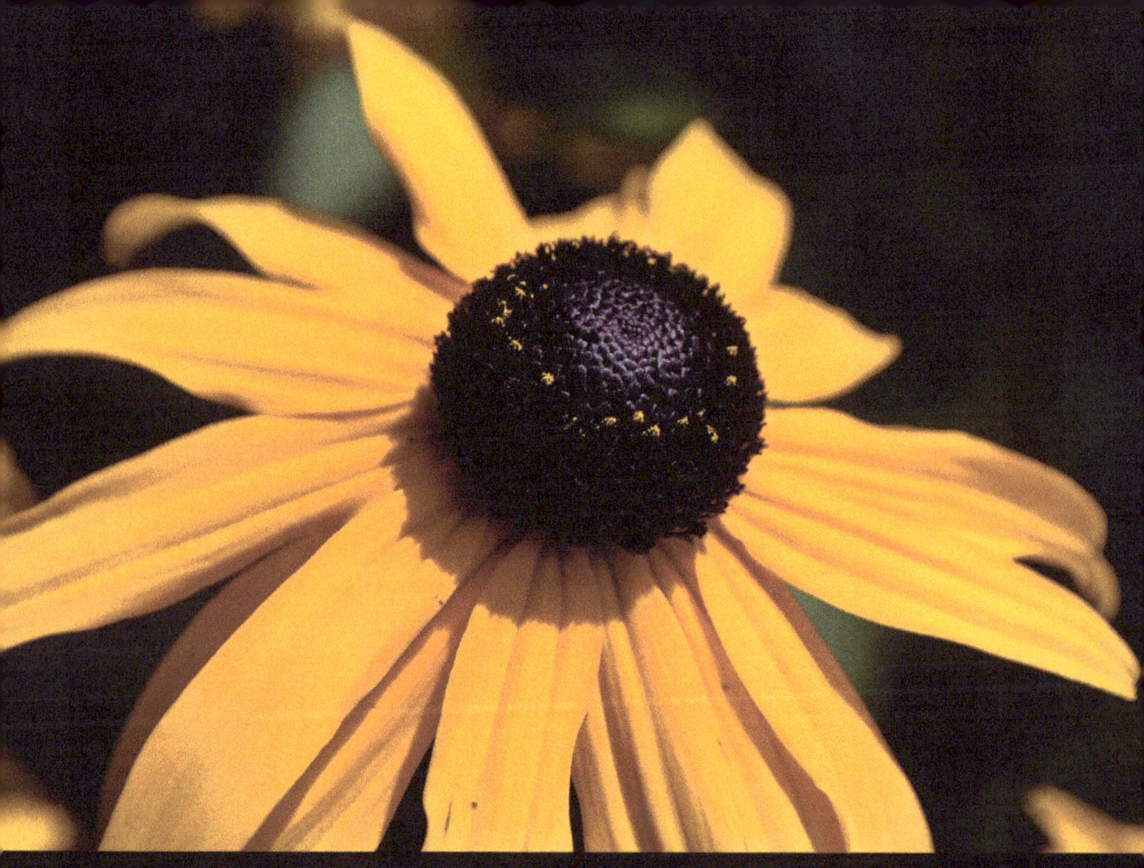

As they stripped away her pollen, bees came less frequently. Black-eyed Susan missed their buzziness but not their over-enthusiastic tickles.

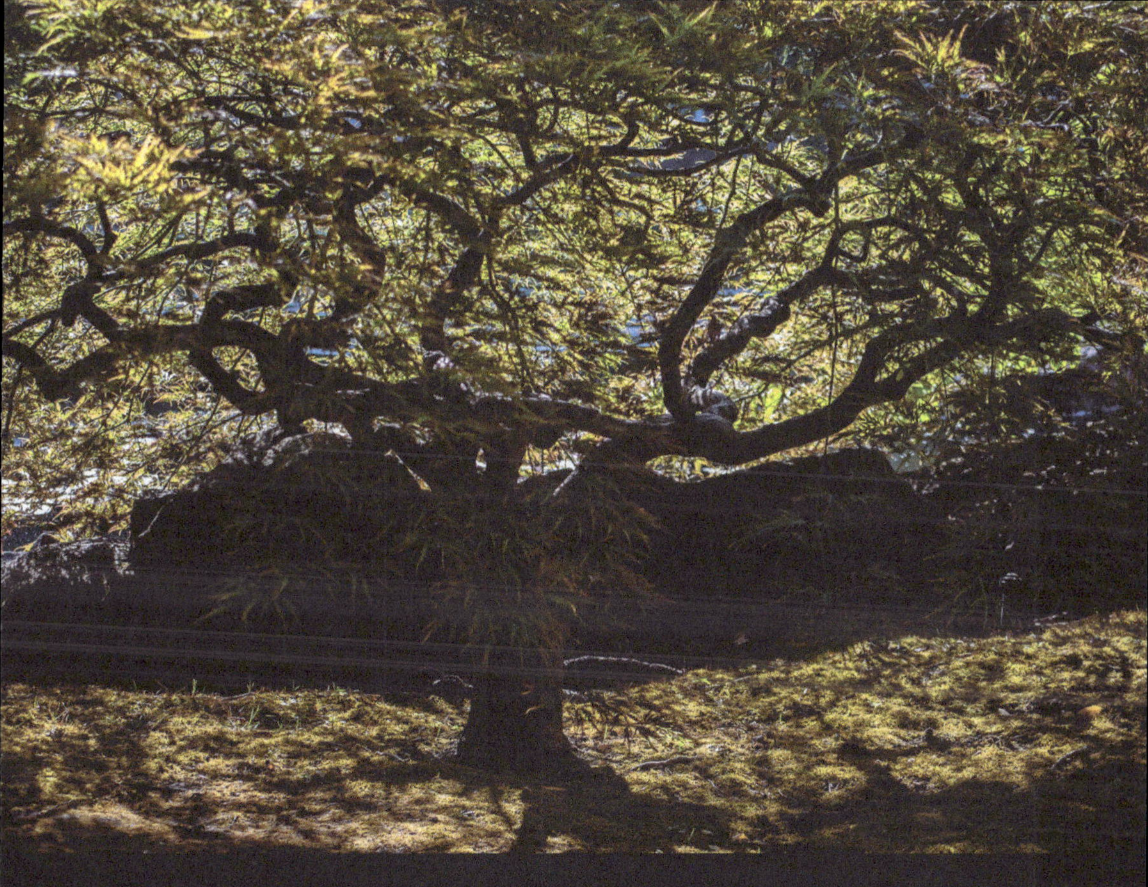

The fairy folk peered out from the shadow of rocks and the shelter of moss. They were stunned by the beauty of the place they had chosen for the annual Faery Folk Ball.

Clouds were perfecting their Bony Fingers imitation. They would know they had mastered it when people on the ground looked up in fear. Apparently they still needed practice.

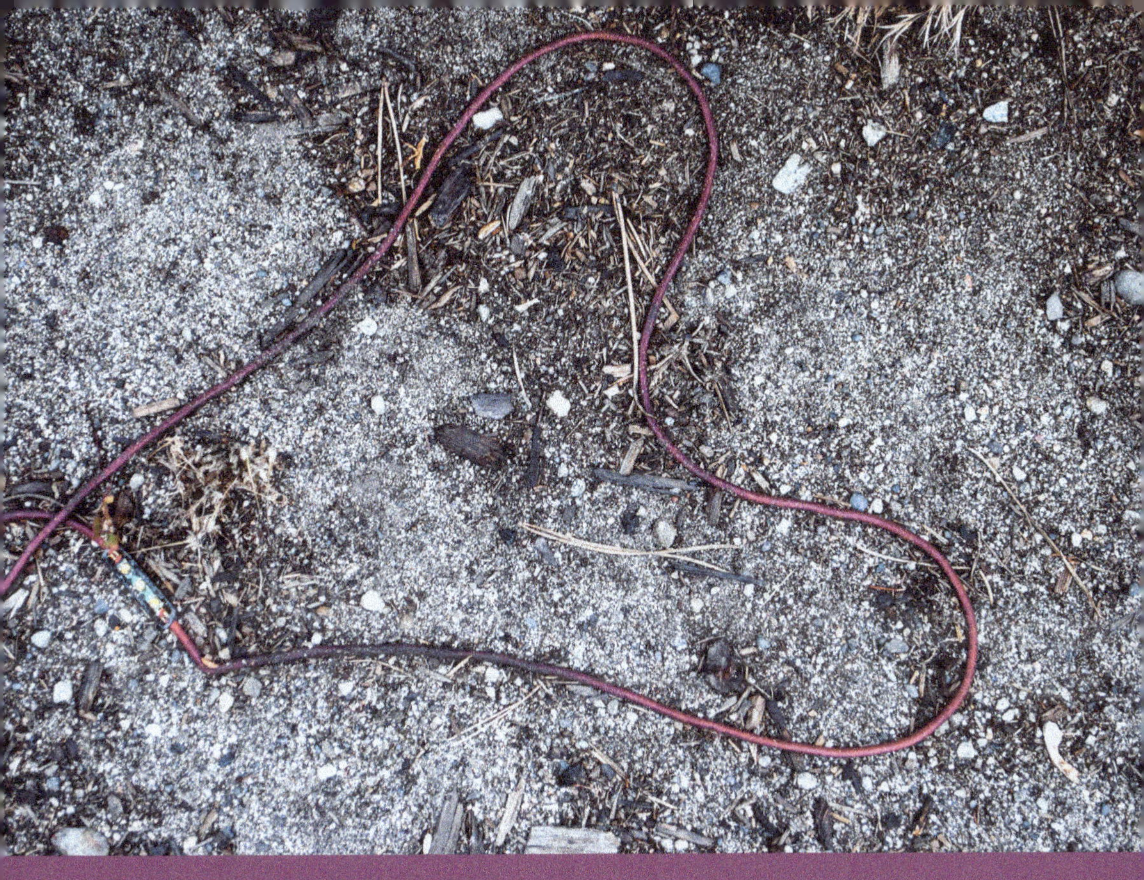

Sometimes love shows up in unexpected places, like the detritus left behind in a demolition site.

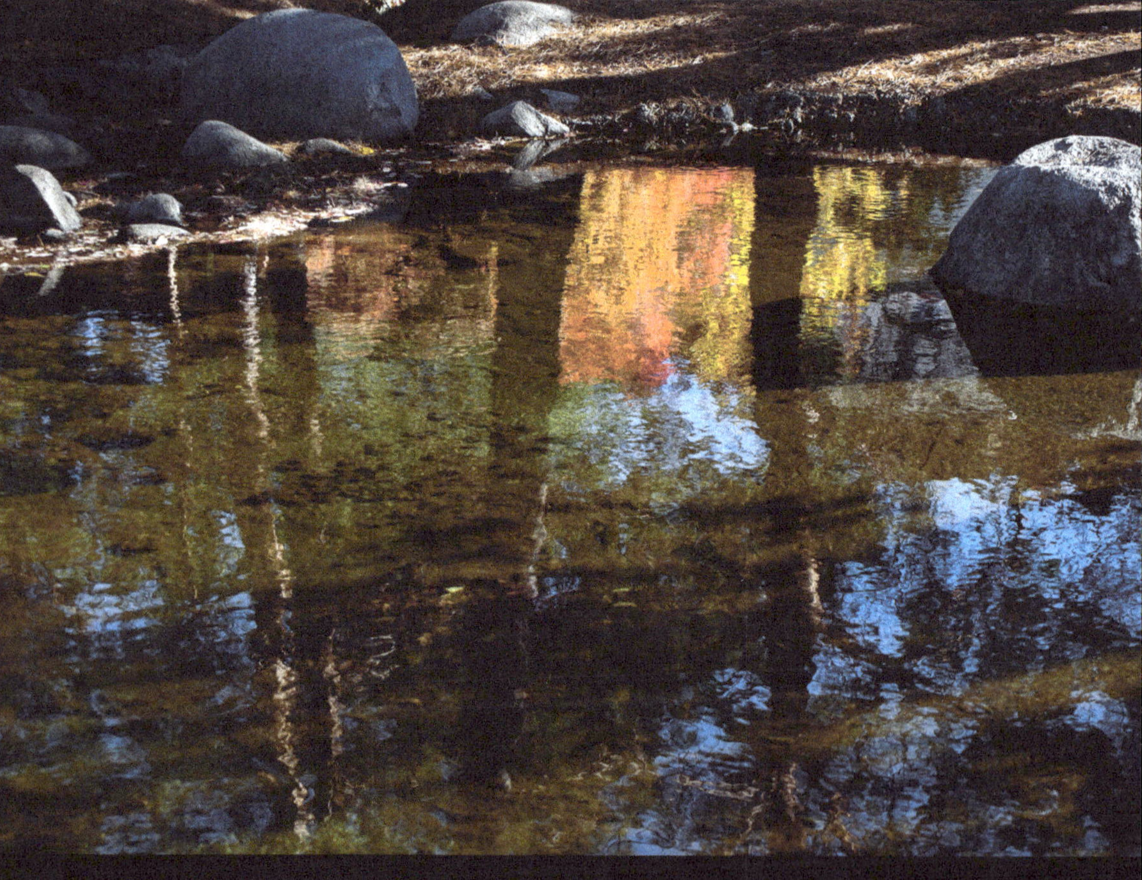

"Come on," said Trees. "It's time for the Autumn Game. Sun, you line up with Leaves. Wind, you make Leaves shimmer, but not too much. Leaves, cast your beauty right here on Water." It all worked out so they hoped someone would photograph them at their best.

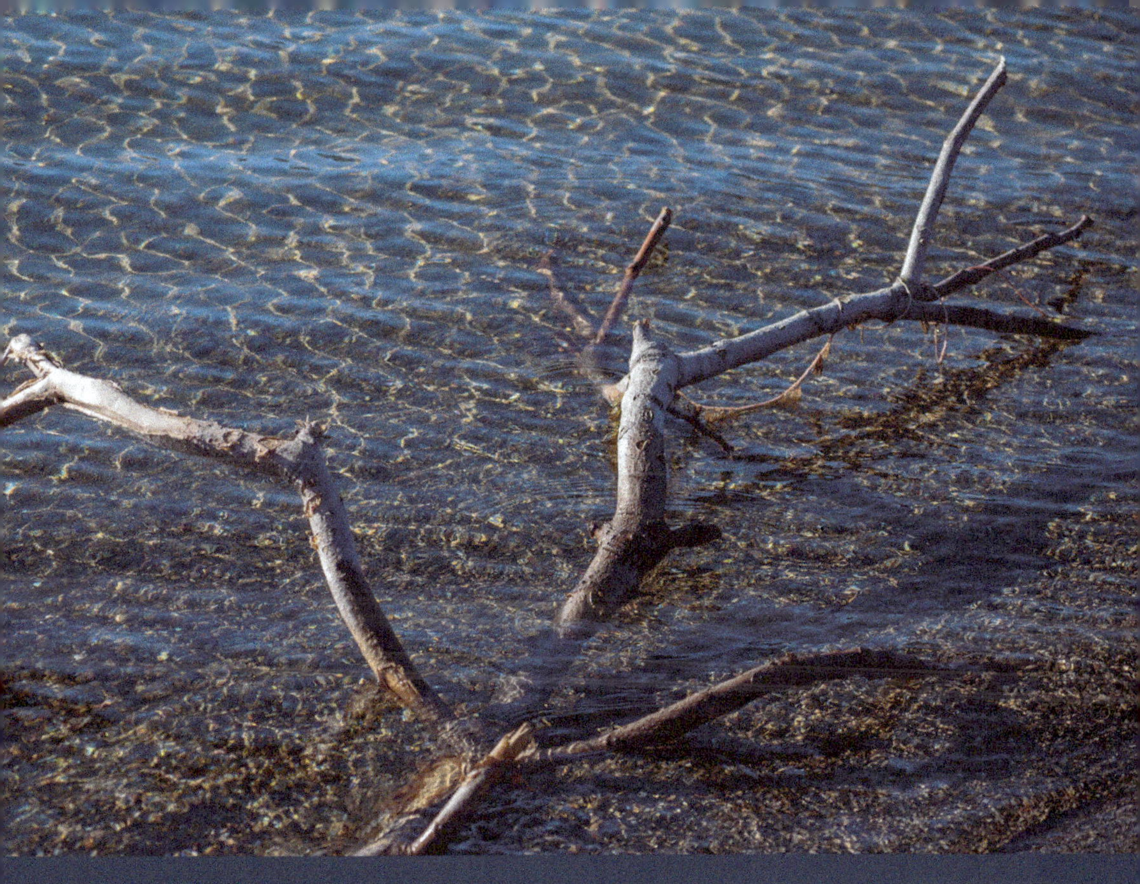

A homeless man was sleeping on the sandy beach.
Branch was thrilled. Maybe this human would have time
to listen to his travel stories. After all, he hadn't always
been a bare, floating derelict, despised by boaters.

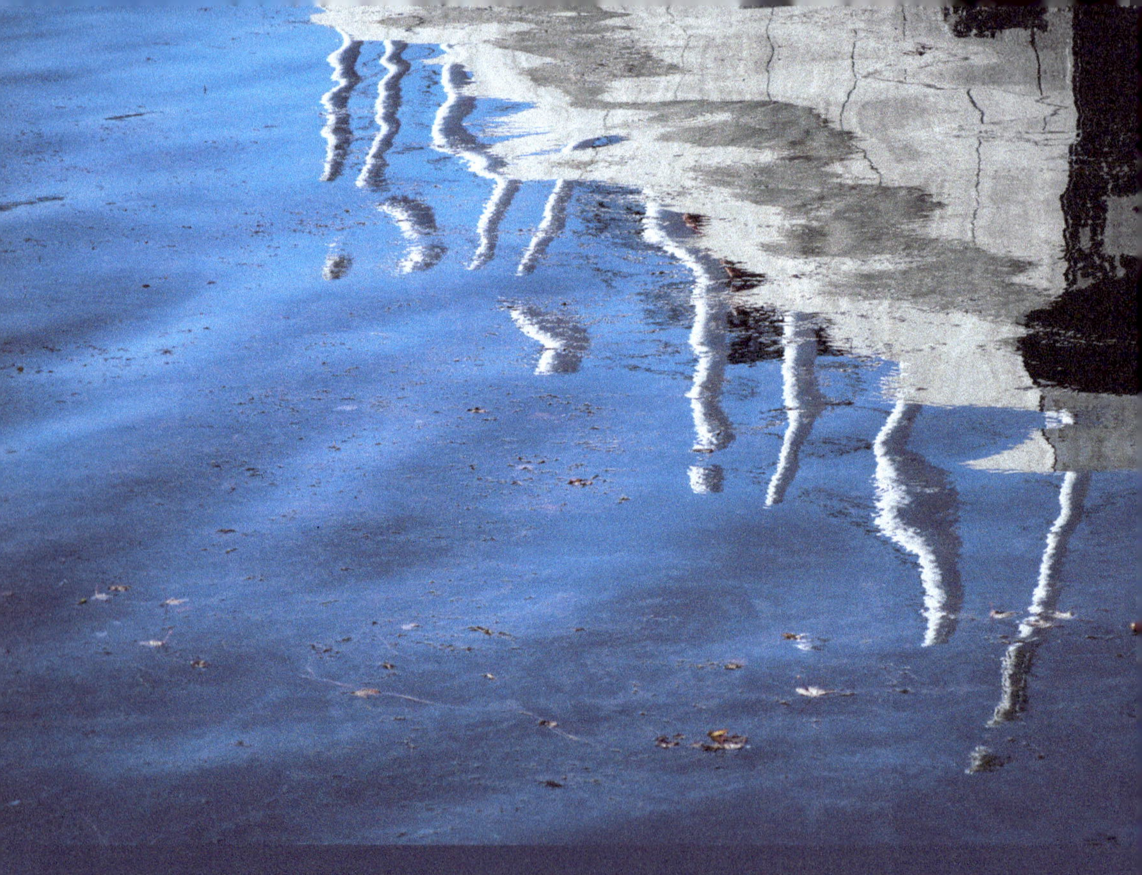

Inspired by the costumed ghouls and zombies they had seen on Hallowe'en, the posts talked Water and Wind into waving their reflections into weird configurations. Who needed a costume when you had helpful friends?

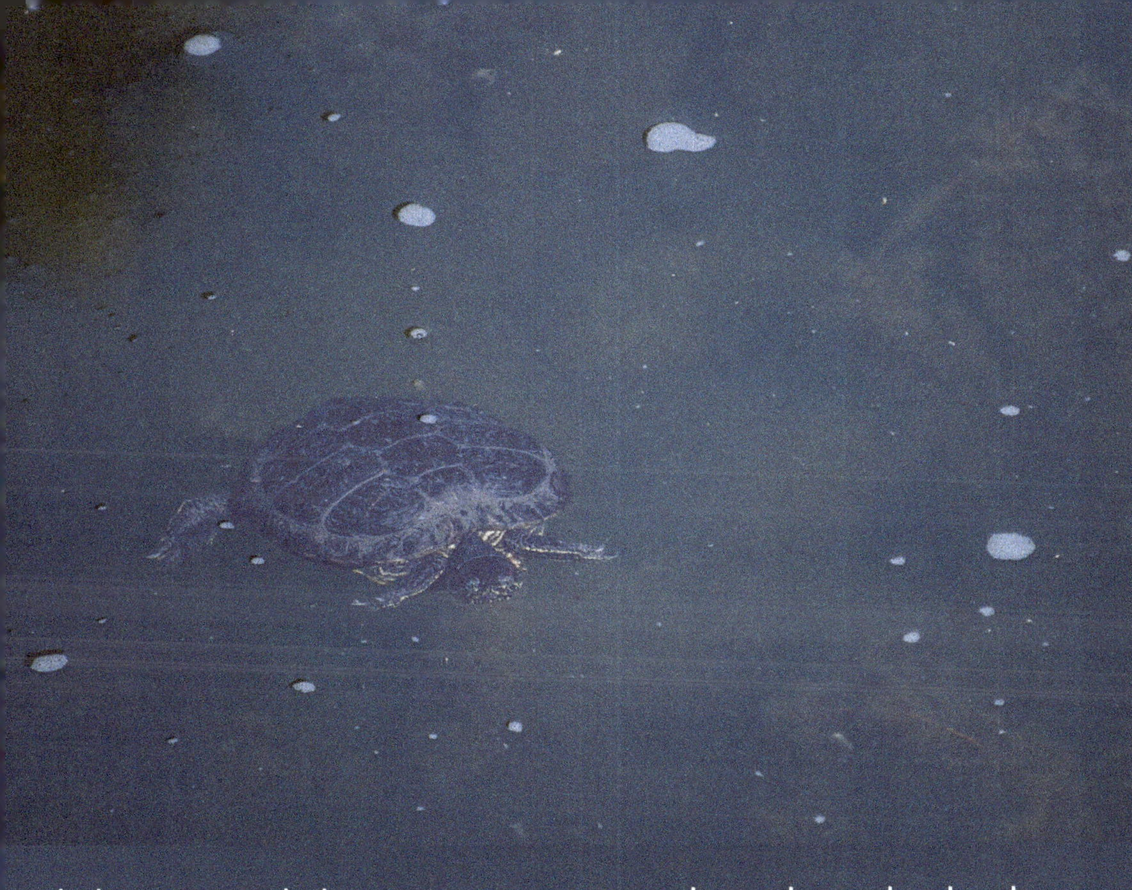

Slider missed the western painted turtles who had
been good friends last year, but he had plenty of
company. The koi kept him entertained with their
flashing colors. The mallards amused him with their
bawdy jokes. He was almost ready for the quiet of
Mud Time.

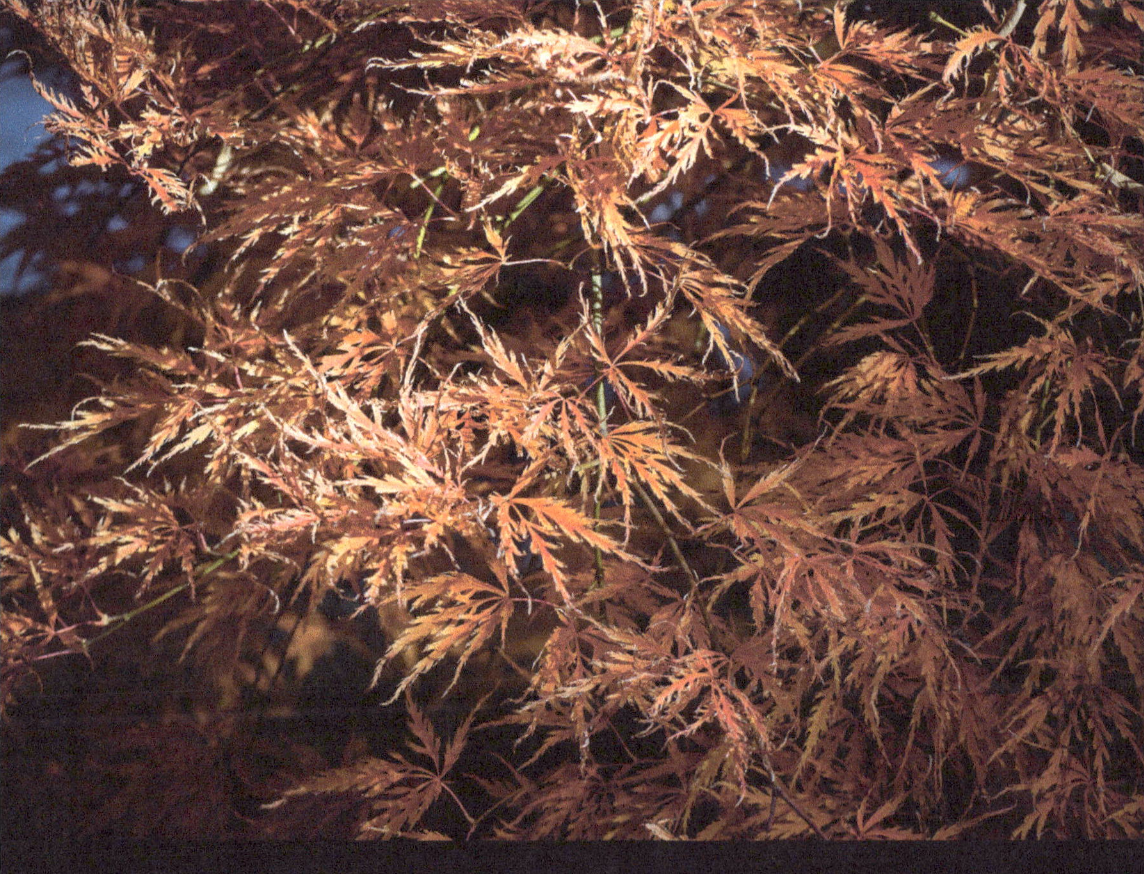

"Do you remember the words?" asked Trunk. The autumn-tinged leaves had never been here before. They had never learned the words. Trunk, who had always been there, tried not to be impatient. "They go like this," he said, "The autumn leaves drift by my window…"

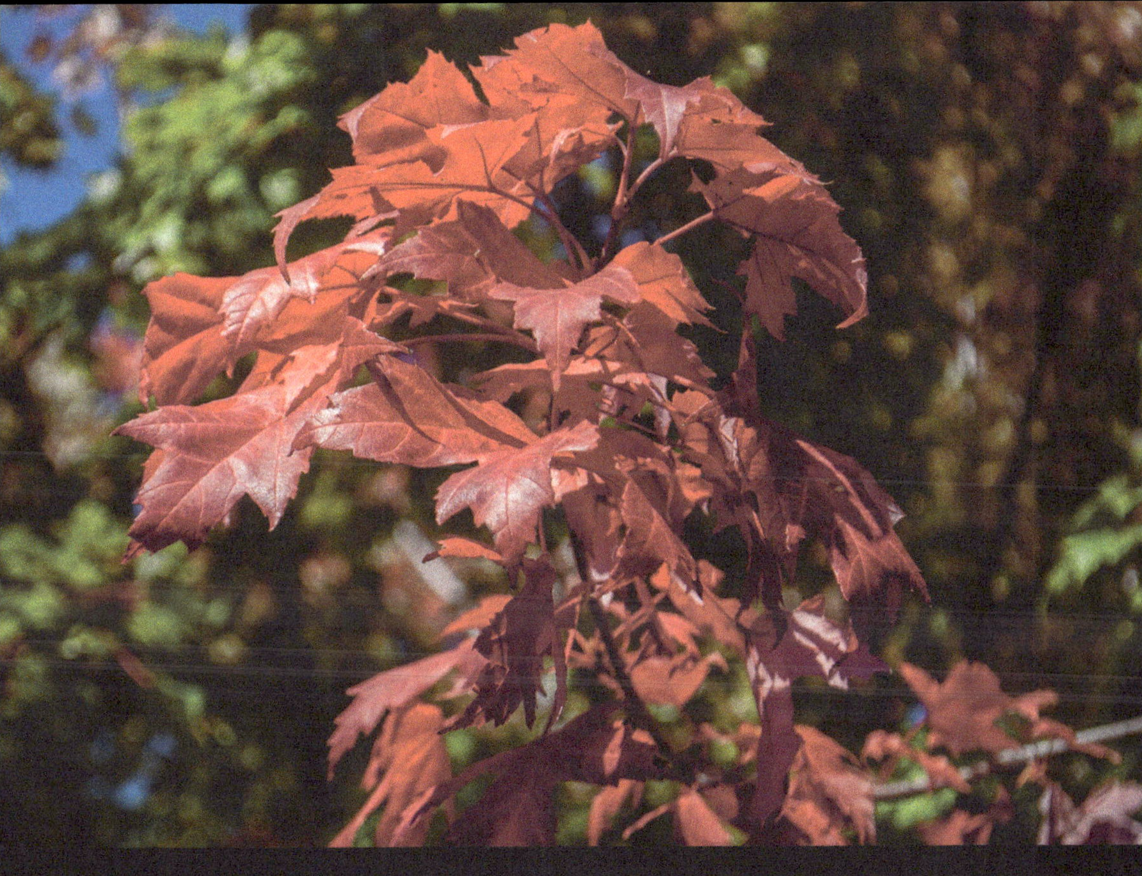

Tree's green leaves were awestruck by the brilliant red among them. They had been worrying about getting old and useless and dropping from their tree. The Reds inspired them to flaunt their incredible ability to change colors before falling.

When the
first boot
shattered his
smooth
surface,
Snow was
irritated. The
second boot
belonged to
a laugher, the
third to a
toddler, and
the fourth to
a singer.
Snow was
enchanted
and hoped
more boots
would come.

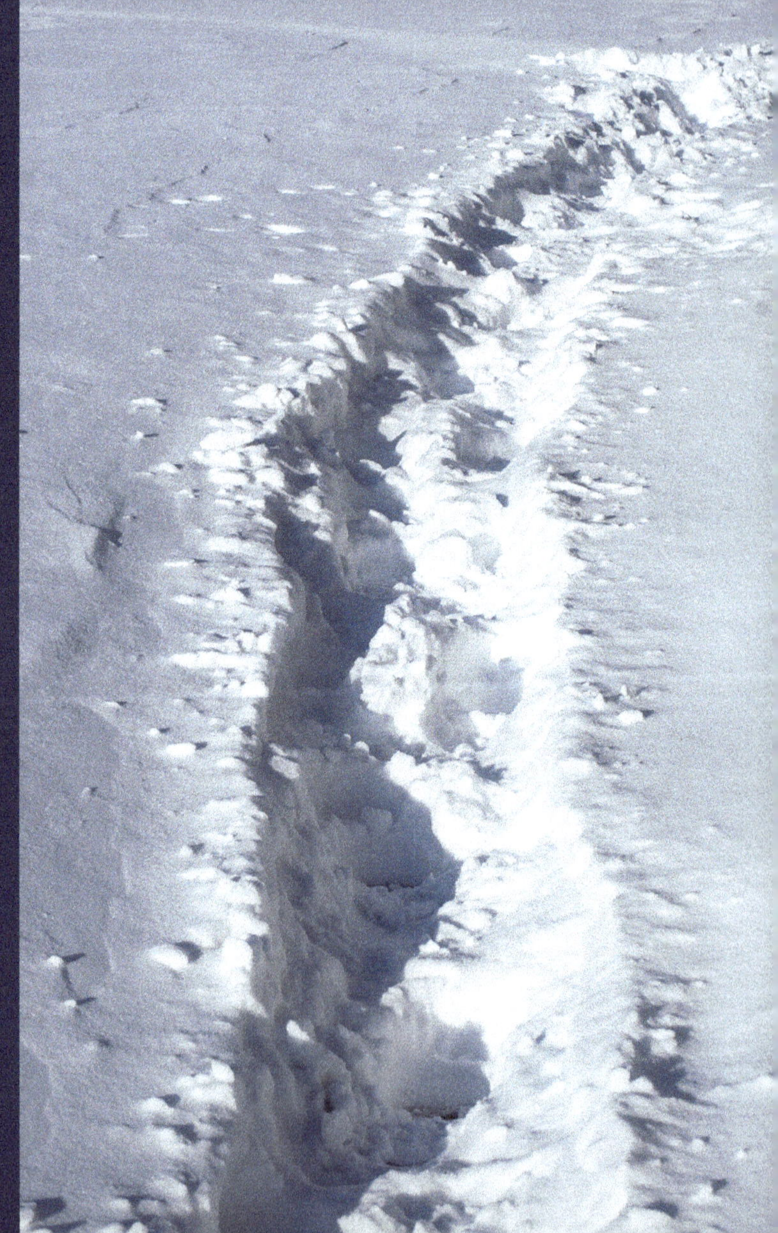

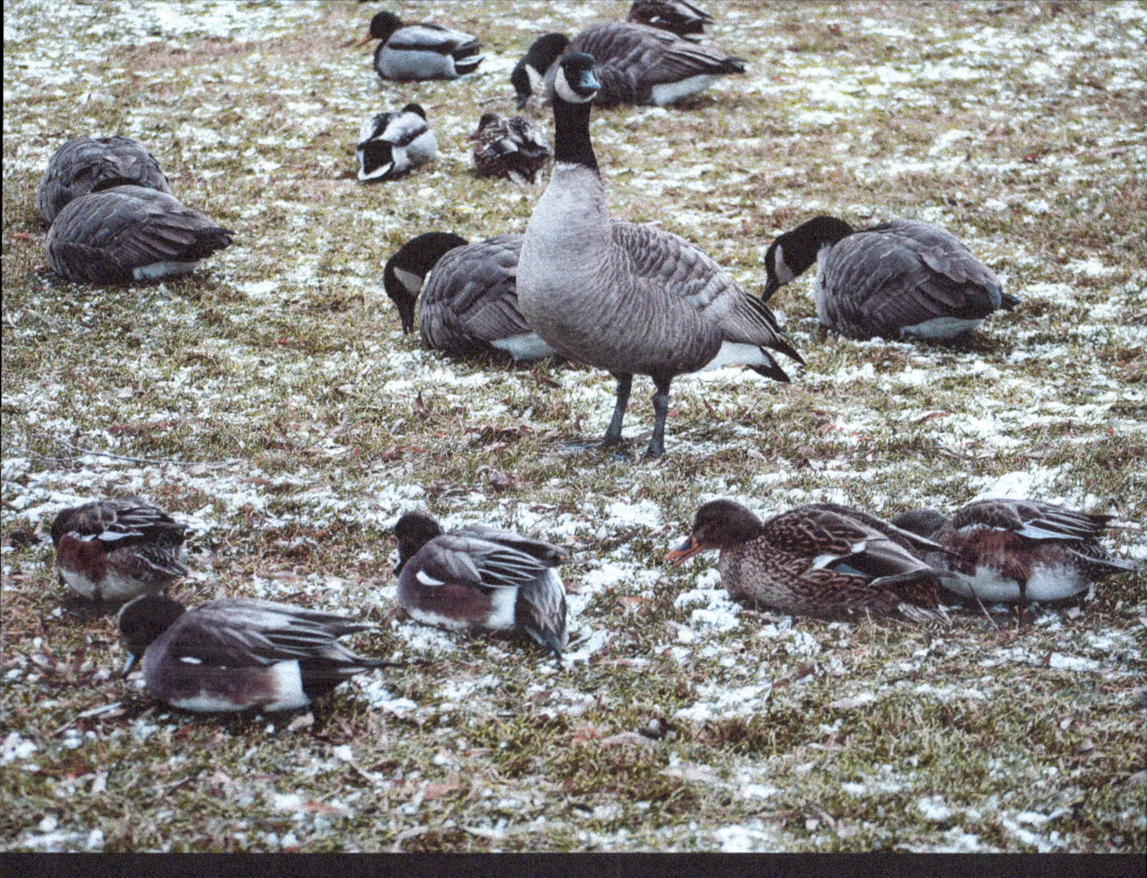

Gander gazed around at the flock depending on his vigilance. "I didn't know about the wigeons and mallards when I signed up for this job," he sighed, but he had to admit they were not much extra work.

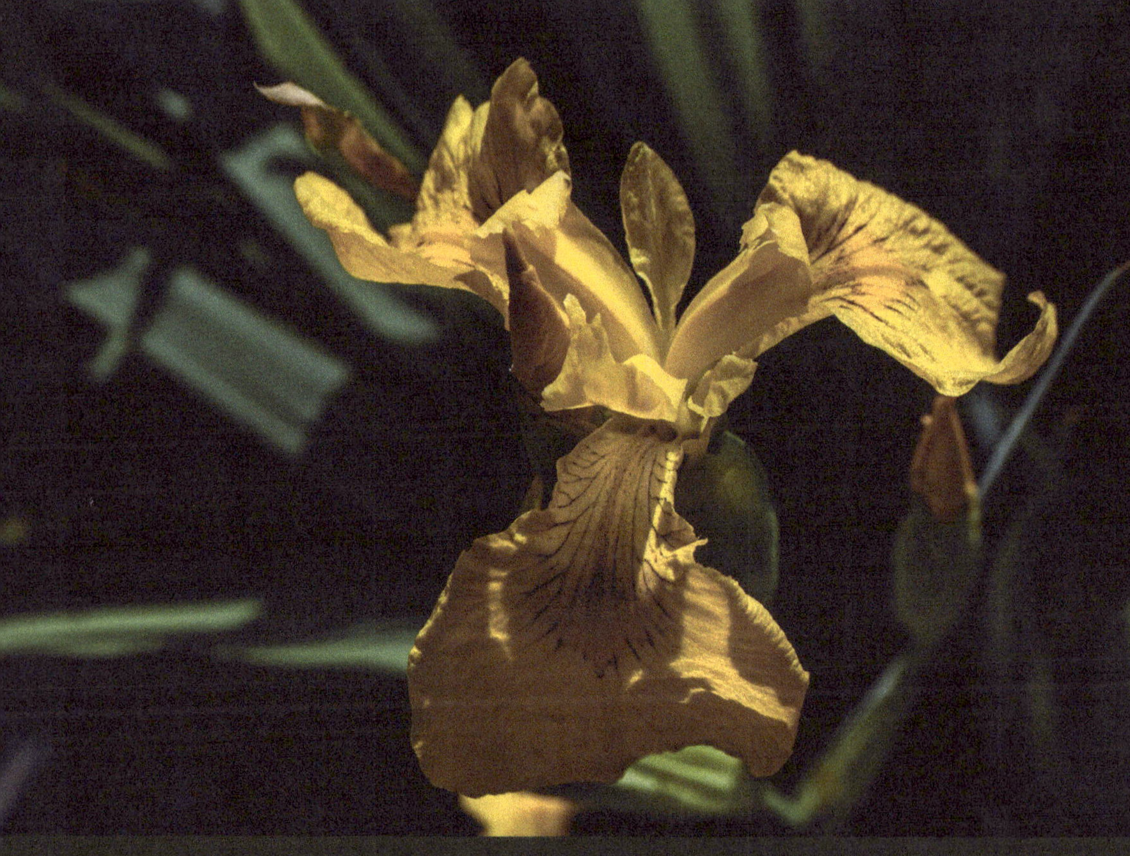

He was doing his best lion imitation and was disappointed when no one took him seriously.

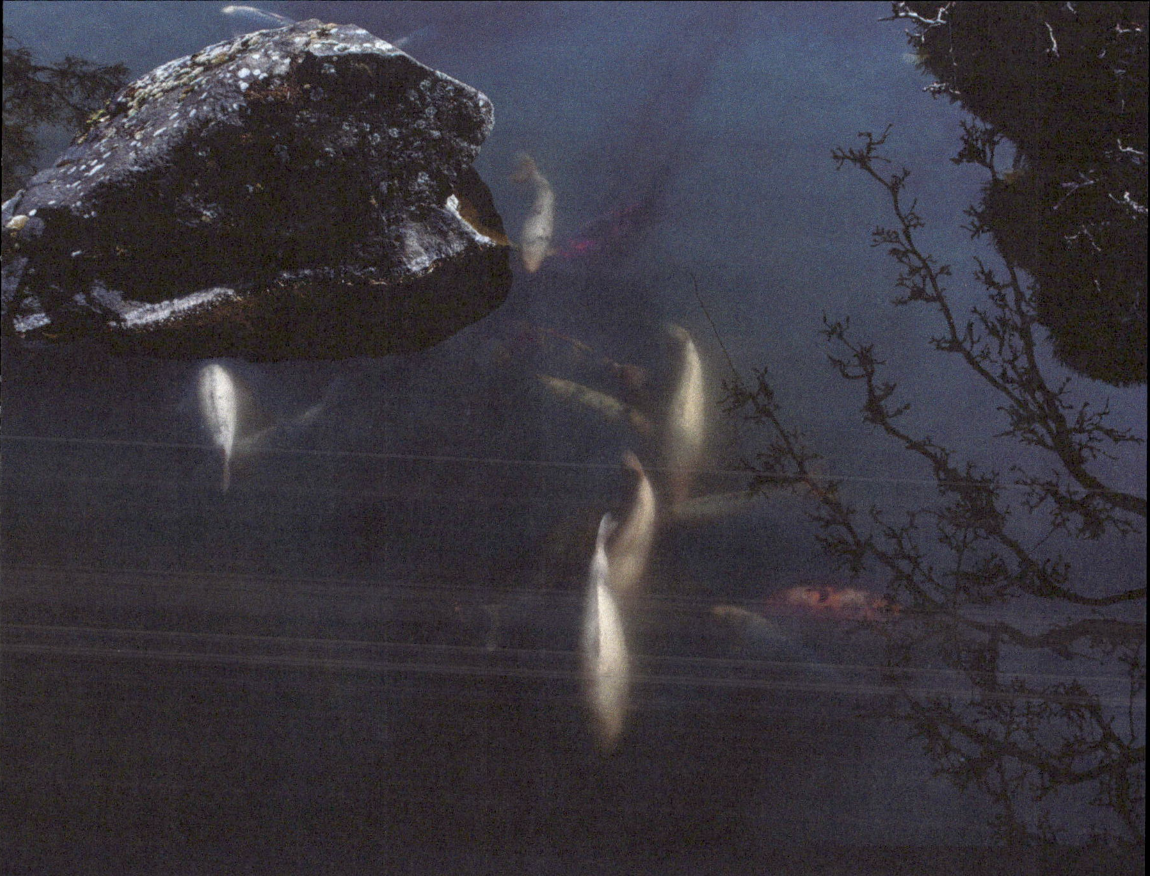

Magic fish swam in the pond. When visitors walked by, they dimmed their brightness. As soon as no one was watching, they glowed once again and gathered to plan the mystery and wonder they would send out into the larger world.

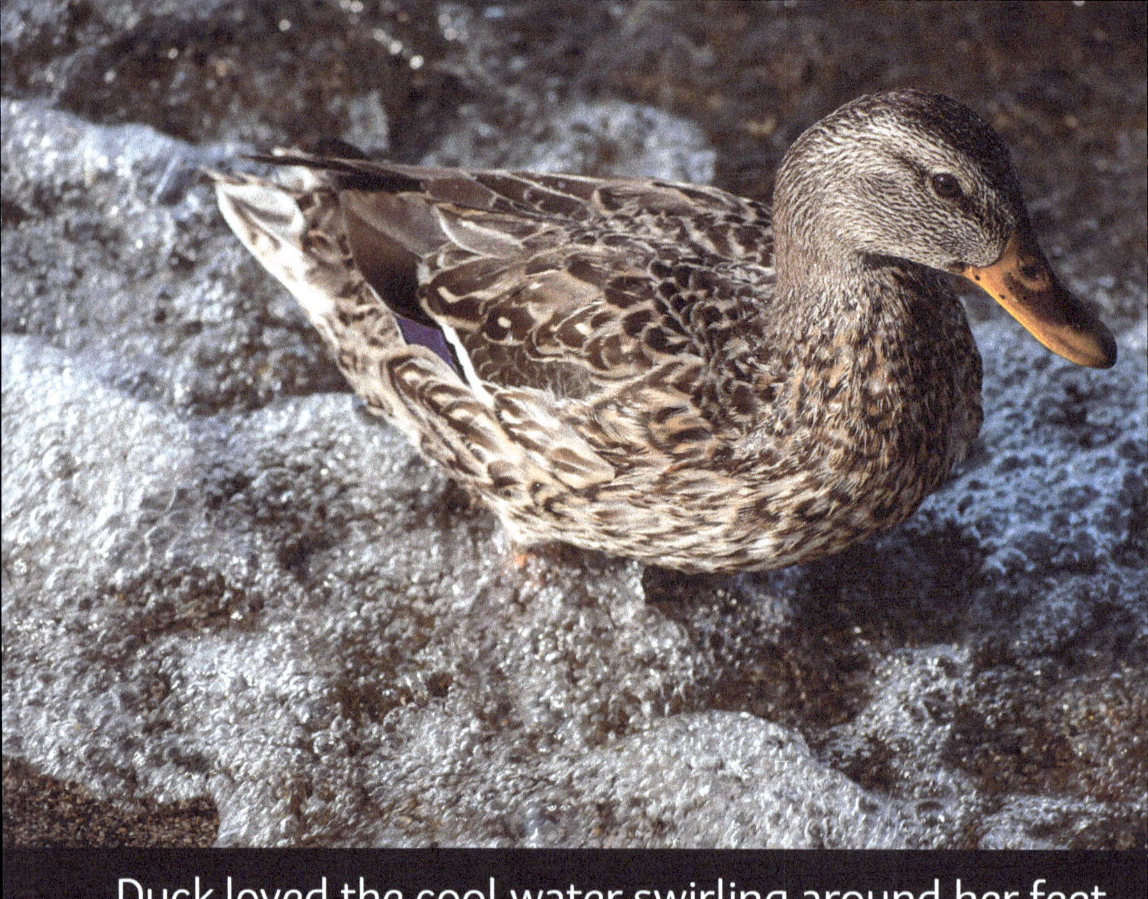

Duck loved the cool water swirling around her feet. She kept herself in fine trim, knowing the time was fast approaching when she would have to decide whether to fly south or tough it out in the cold. Either way, she would be prepared.

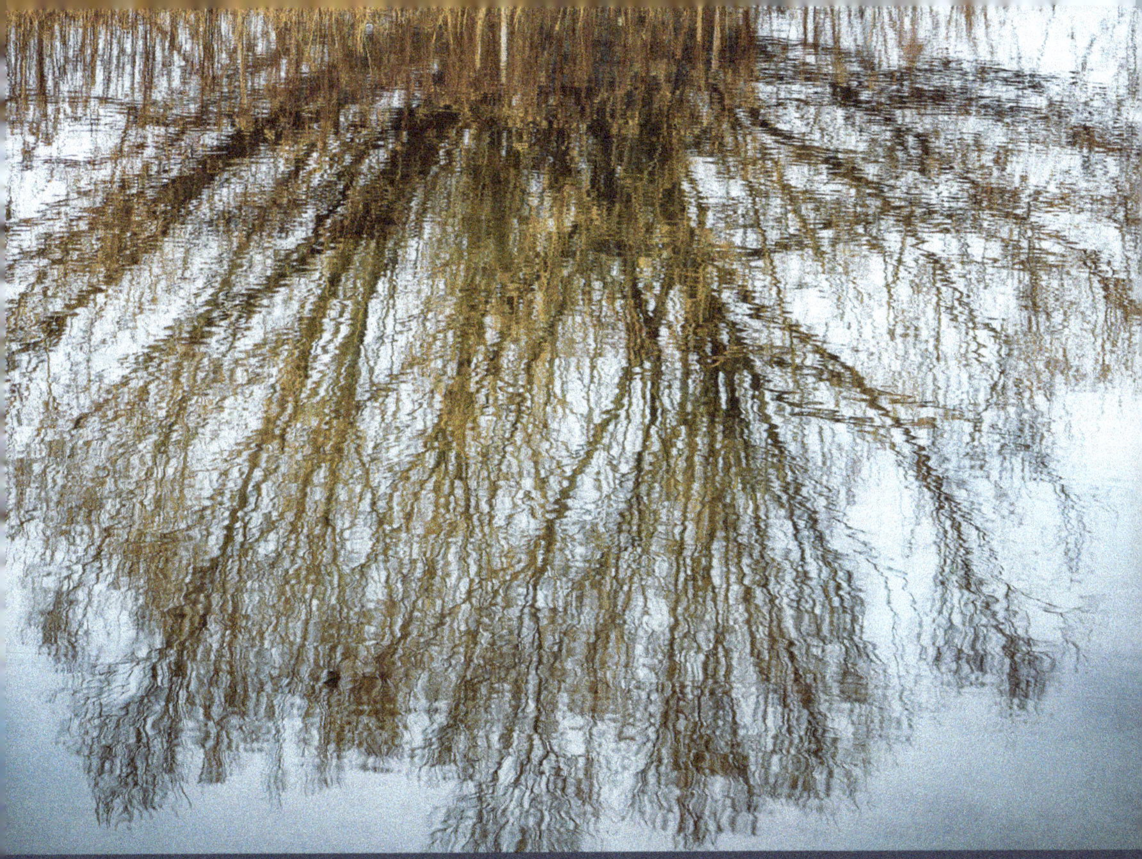

"Stop tickling the water, Breeze," said Willow. "You're messing up my reflection." Water rippled with laughter, knowing something Willow kept forgetting, that a little "messing up" made life so much more interesting.

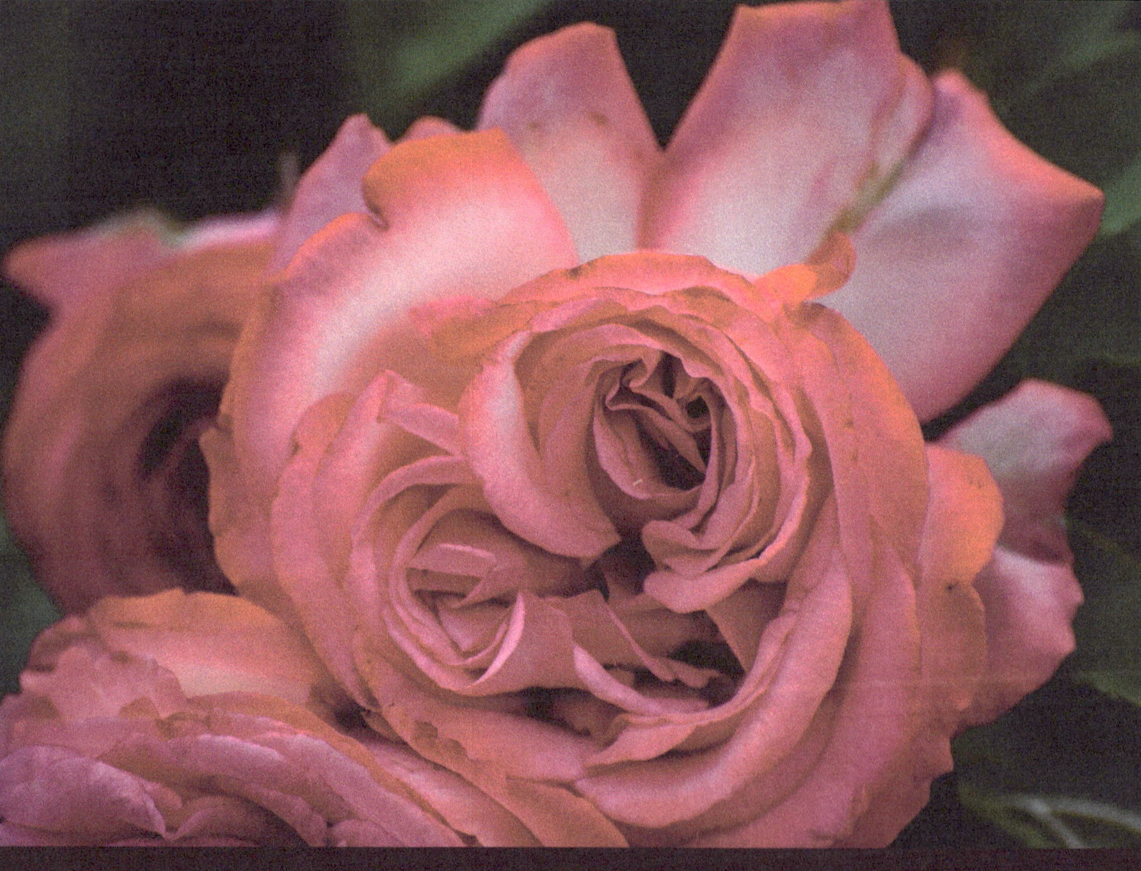

They grew as identical twins until a halfling opened insistent petals beside them. They welcomed her, although she was only half formed. What she lacked in symmetry, she made up for in sweetness.

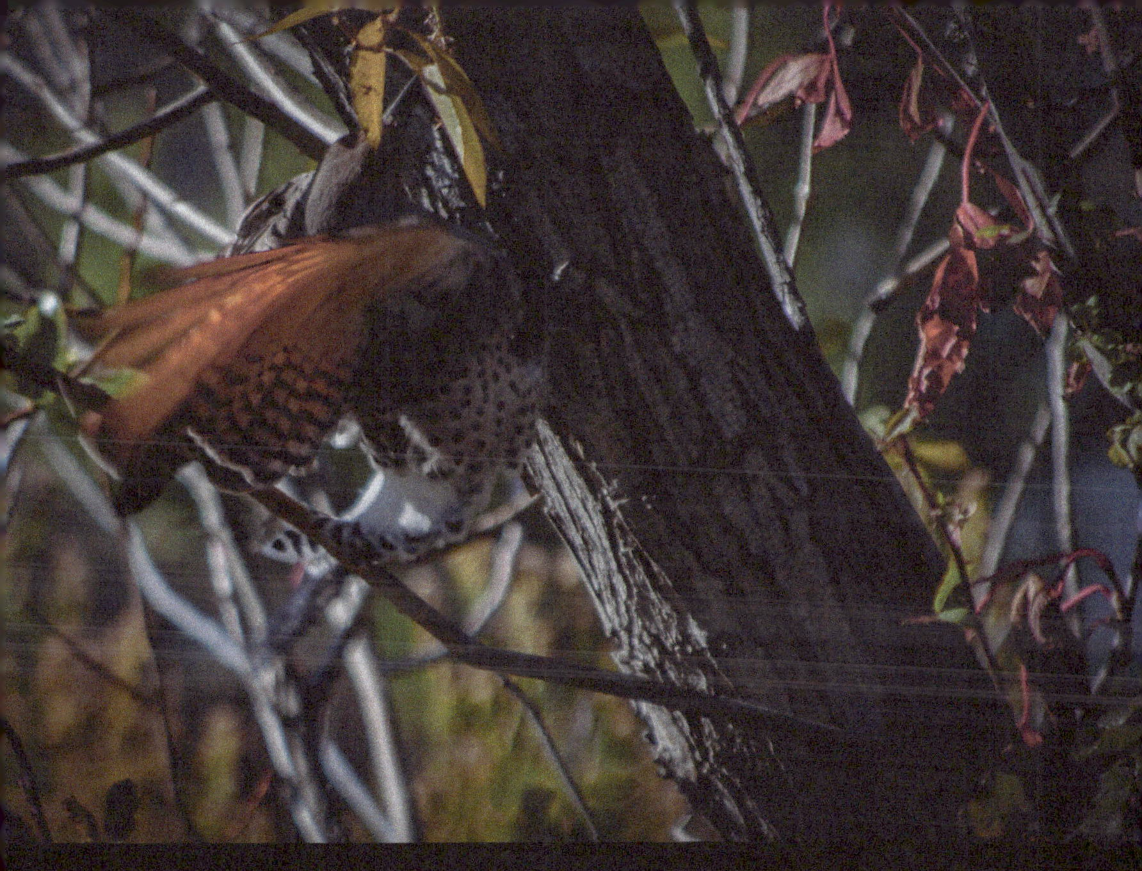

Flicker was pleased the humans walked by just as
he made one of his most acrobatic moves. Some
of them were a most appreciative audience. As for
the others, he would tap on their houses and
laugh raucously.

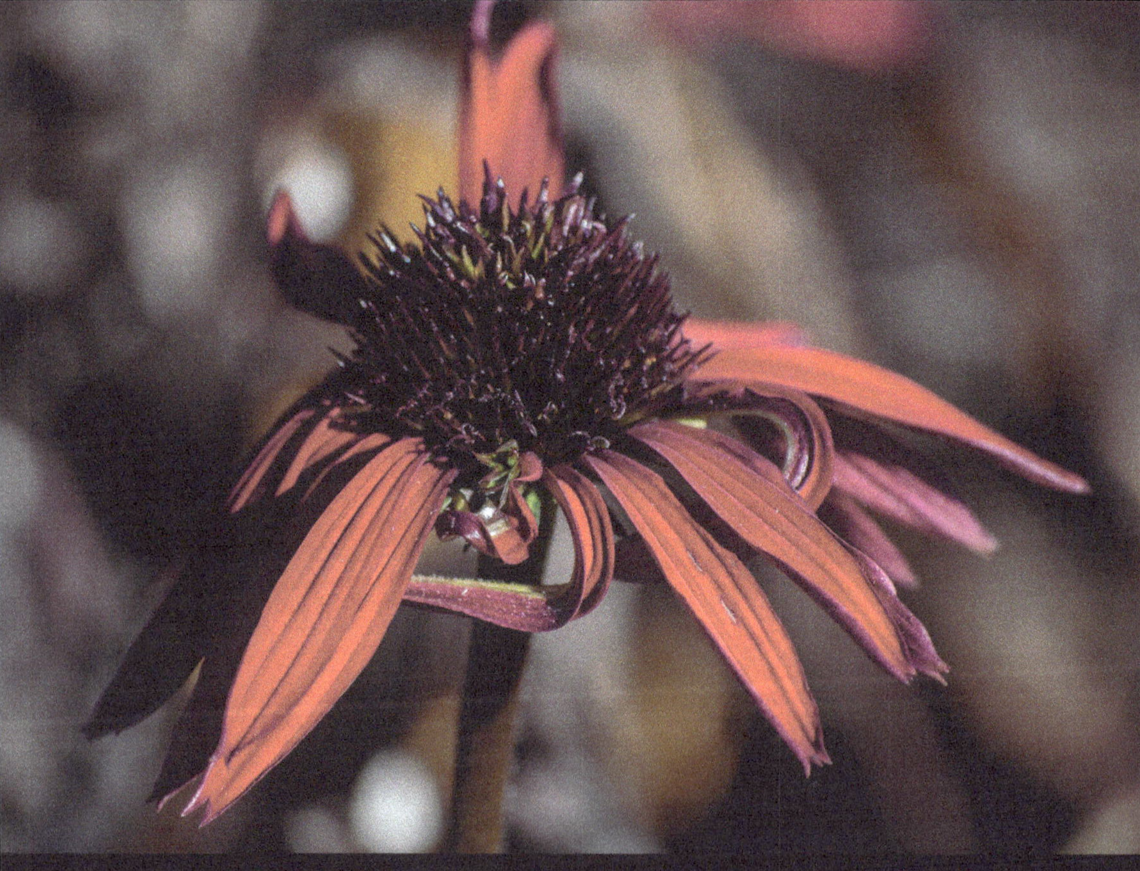

When her petals were young, Coneflower was a ballet diva in a brilliant, red tutu. Now she was a flamenco dancer, dramatically flinging her petals in the wind.

Credits

Fonts used on cover and some interior pages: Canvas, Saltash, Sun Kissed. Font used in stories: Bw Surco. Logo font: Ed's Market. Hands on dedication page are from Pixabay. All other fonts and graphic elements are licensed through DesignCuts.

Text and photographs by Cathryn Wellner. The book was designed in Photoshop.

Thank you to the creative people who designed the unique fonts and elements incorporated in this book. I continually learn from you.

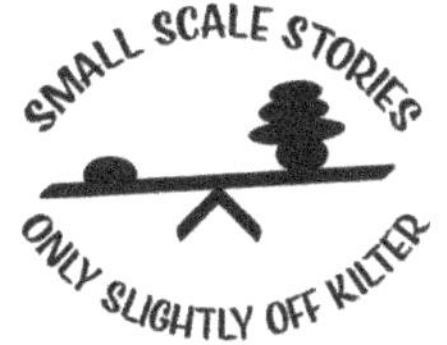

Lorem Ipsum

ABOUT THE AUTHOR

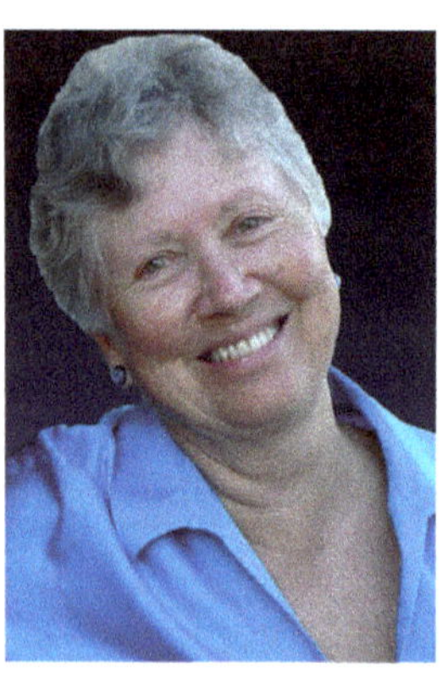

Cathryn Wellner is a writer, photographer and storyteller living in Kelowna, British Columbia, Canada. Her recent books include:

Small Scale Stories series (*That Tree Talked to Me, Parts of Me Are Still Amazing, The Disappearing Pumpkin Choir, In the Shelter of Each Other, Your Task Is to Be Admired, In the Country of Plastic, I'll Tell You a Story, Excited and Kind of Scared*)

Essay collections (*Hope Wins & Feisty Aging*)
In the Hug of Hills
Millie's Foster Family children's series (*Millie's Feathered Foster Family, Turkey Baby and the Hungry Hawk, Turkey Baby Finds Her Magic*)

You can find links to these and her other books at cathrynwellner.com. Contact her at cathryn@cathrynwellner.com or 778-478-2760. Her photographs can be found on her Web site, as well as on Facebook and Instagram.

BE A BOOK REVIEW ANGEL

If you enjoyed this book, please post a review on Amazon or Goodreads. Share it with friends and rave about it on social media. You can contact the author at cathryn@cathrynwellner.com.

Authors rely on their readers to help spread the word about books they like. People who review books are special kinds of reader angels. I guarantee when you review this book, or any other book that has given you pleasure in any way, you'll feel those wings poking out your back. Look closely in the mirror, and you might even see a halo.

www.ingramcontent.com/pod-product-compliance
Lightning Source LLC
Chambersburg PA
CBHW041050050726
47599CB00018B/2096